BACKGAMMON

Robin Clay is the well known authority on Backgammon, whose clear and concise introduction to the game is based on many years of playing experience. He now runs a Backgammon club in his area, from which many accomplished players have emerged, and was a finalist in the 1977 British Open Championship.

TEACH YOURSELF BOOKS

BACKGAMMON

R. A. Clay

TEACH YOURSELF BOOKS
Hodder and Stoughton

First printed 1977
Second impression 1978

Copyright © *1977*
Puzzle Co. Ltd.

This volume is published in the U.S.A. by David McKay Company Inc., 750 Third Avenue, New York, N.Y. 10017

ISBN 0 340 22233 6

Printed in Great Britain for Hodder and Stoughton Paperbacks, a division of Hodder and Stoughton Ltd, Mill Road, Dunton Green, Sevenoaks, Kent (Editorial Office, 47 Bedford Square, London WC1 3DP) by Richard Clay (The Chaucer Press), Ltd, Bungay Suffolk

Contents

Preface

The recent dramatic rise in the popularity of backgammon is no cause for wonder. What is remarkable is that it did not occur earlier, for the game has all the elements of success: it is exciting, compulsive, quick to play, and with a nice balance between chance and skill.

To many people, backgammon projects an image of the 'beautiful-people' casino scene on the one hand, and Greek café life on the other. This would not be a false picture, but it would only be a small part of a much larger canvas. Backgammon is indeed popular in the big gaming clubs and in its probable birthplace, the Mediterranean lands; but it is now played, without benefit of media coverage, in unnumbered homes and clubs in Britain and America, and indeed all over the world.

Backgammon has not only become popular; it has become fashionable, and perhaps that is no bad thing. Many people with little interest in indoor games have been encouraged to take up backgammon and have been seized by its appeal.

It was inevitable that the sudden boom gave birth, often premature, to a large family of beginners' books. *Teach Yourself Backgammon* is a clear, considered and complete interpretation of this fascinating game. It has been worth waiting for.

London, October 1976

David Pritchard
Editor, *Games & Puzzles*

Introduction

Welcome to backgammon. Just about 50 centuries ago, at the time of Abraham, men were playing a game that is very similar to modern backgammon, and they have played it ever since.

A game that survives 5000 years, largely unchanged, and is still played by millions of people, must have some unique and fascinating features.

At first sight backgammon appears to be a deceptively simple game of chance, and indeed a 10-year-old child can be taught to play it as a simple game of luck in 30 minutes. Yet the problems of strategy, position and timing are always a matter of dispute, even amongst the top players of the world.

In this one game are combined the qualities of many of the world's most popular games. The backgammon player, must, like the poker player, make the agonising choice of accepting or refusing a doubling of the stakes, but unlike poker there are no hidden hands, and therefore far less bluff—you see your opponent's men and every move he makes.

Bridge, like backgammon, has doubles and re-doubles, but in bridge you are forced to accept, and if your opponent makes an error of play you cannot re-double after bidding has closed and play commenced. In backgammon you have the choice to refuse or accept a double, or if fortune and skill favour you, the right to re-double as the game proceeds.

Like chess, the player may sacrifice a man to gain a strategic advantage, and with every throw of the dice a choice must be made—to attack, run, block or sacrifice.

Like the craps player, the backgammon player must understand the throws of the dice, but in backgammon they are more varied and complex. The craps player is concerned only with the totals of the two dice, giving 11 different combinations. In backgammon each throw has three values, the value of each individual die, and the combined total, giving rise to 36 permutations of the dice.

With contract bridge the luck element is virtually settled as soon as the cards have been dealt, and you must frequently play out a game with little hope of any change of fortune once the bidding is complete. With backgammon, luck can spill out of the dice cups with every throw, and even the most formidable situations can be reversed with one lucky throw.

This mixture of elements from the world's most popular games makes backgammon one of the most exciting games to play, whether it is played as a simple game of luck with a child, or as a fascinating game of skill, cunning and strategy by experts. No two games are ever identical, and only rarely does a game last more than 7 minutes.

Like so many games, backgammon is a warfare game in miniature. Each player moves his men around the dagger-like spikes of the board with dice throws; your army of men must clash with those of your opponent, set ambushes and blockades, capture enemy men, and finally pass through his ranks to reach your final objective—your home board, where, in order to win, you must remove all your men from the board with dice throws.

Like the Japanese game of Go, many players take so much delight in knocking an opponent's man off the board that they lose sight of the final objective. In backgammon, unlike most games, a man 'captured' on the way is not 'dead'; instead it must re-enter the game at a point furthest away from its home board, and run the gauntlet of your army to get back. This may sound like a major reverse for your opponent, but if this man hits one of your men just at a moment when you are weakening yourself by taking your men off the board, your winning position can be totally reversed.

The sudden changes of fortune keep the players tense and excited, and it requires the greatest skill to arrange your men to cope not only with your own unexpected dice throws, but also those of your opponent. No description can do justice to this game; you must play it, and find out for yourself.

This book is written for the complete beginner, but you will find in it instructive and helpful advice to suit anyone who is still below the expert level.

1 Beginners' Basics

Backgammon is a very easy game to learn. This chapter gives the rules, explanations and instructions. As with all games learning this part is a little dull, but as you move on through the book you will get into the fun and excitement of the game.

Equipment

To play you must have the basic equipment, which consists of:

1 A backgammon board.
2 Thirty men, 15 of each colour.
3 2 pairs of dice.
4 Two dice shakers.
5 A doubling cube.

and finally an opponent with whom to play.

Before you read any further get out your backgammon board, open it on the table in front of you and set out and follow every situation as you read about it. You cannot make any real progress if you read this book like a novel. Only practice will make you a proficient player.

The board and starting positions

Diagram 1 shows the board before the men have been laid out for play. It consists of 24 dagger-like spikes known as 'points' of alternate colour. They can be red and white, black and white or any two contrasting colours. Neither the shape nor the colour are of importance; the points are merely used to count the

DIAGRAM 1

BLACK

12 11 10 9 8 7 6 5 4 3 2 1

BLACK OUTER BOARD

BLACK HOME BOARD

BLACK BAR POINT

THE BAR

WHITE BAR POINT

WHITE OUTER BOARD

WHITE HOME BOARD

12 11 10 9 8 7 6 5 4 3 2 1

WHITE

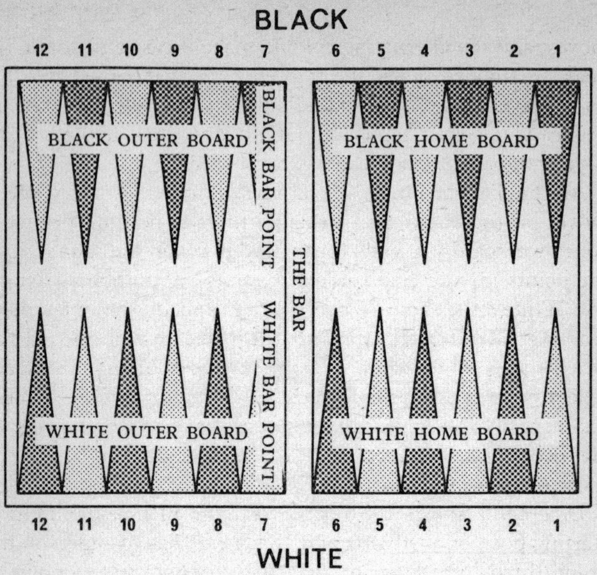

DIAGRAM 2

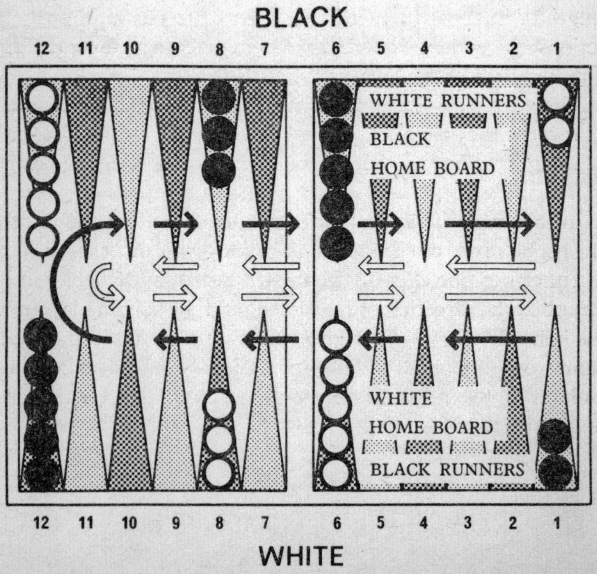

BLACK

12 11 10 9 8 7 6 5 4 3 2 1

WHITE RUNNERS
BLACK
HOME BOARD

WHITE
HOME BOARD

BLACK RUNNERS

12 11 10 9 8 7 6 5 4 3 2 1

WHITE

moves, and the alternating colours make it easier to count. The board is divided down the middle by a strip called the 'bar'. Each player has a 'home board' and an 'outer board'. The side nearest you is your home and outer board, the side further away is your opponent's home and outer board.

All the diagrams in this book carry numbers to designate the moves on the board, and although there is nothing printed on your own board you will always need to retain the numbering of the points in your mind. Black's points are numbered 1 to 12, and White's the same. When a move is made the notation will read B12–W7, which means that a man has been moved from Black's 12 point to White's 7 point, a total of 6 points, or spaces. The 7 point is always known as the 'bar' point. The colours of the men, like the colours of the points, have no significance, and are necessarily different only to distinguish your men from those of your opponent.

Diagram 2 shows the board with the men laid out in the starting position ready for play. Each side has five men on his 6 point, three on the 8 point, five on the opponent's 12 point and two on the opponent's 1 point. The two men on the opponent's 1 point are known as 'runners', and they have to travel the entire length of the board to get home. Play proceeds in opposite directions; the white and black arrows in diagram 2 show the direction in which each player moves his men.

There are two different starting positions for backgammon. You can either have the home board on your right (*diagram 2*) or the mirror image with the home board on your left (*diagram 3*).

In this book the layout with the home board on the right will always be used, but from the beginning you must learn to play in either position. Set out your own board, and when you have absorbed the direction of movement and the starting layout with the home board on your right, walk round the table and study it from your opponent's viewpoint. You will find that you are looking at the mirror image and that your opponent has his home board on his left.

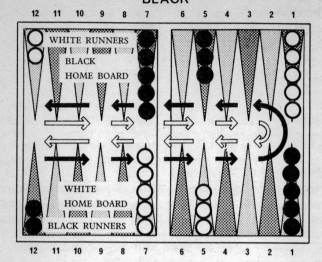

DIAGRAM 3

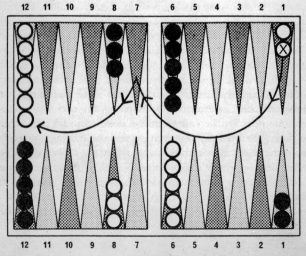

DIAGRAM 4

The objective

To win at backgammon you must move your men round the board (in the direction shown by the marker arrows in *diagram 2*) from your opponent's home board to his outer board, onto your outer board and into your inner board. Once all your men are in your home board you start a process known as 'bearing off', whereby you remove all the men from the board with throws of the dice. The winner is the first player to remove all his men from the board.

Starting the game

If there is any dispute between the players over the choice of colour, or direction of movement, the matter is resolved by each throwing one die, the player throwing the higher die having choice of colour and direction of movement. To start the game each player throws one die. If they each throw the same number the process is repeated until one player throws a higher number than his opponent, and he has the opening move. His first move is determined by the two dice just thrown, his own and his opponent's. Thereafter each player plays alternately, casting both his dice and moving accordingly.

Moving the men

Each player has thrown one die for the opening move, and let us assume the result is that Black throws a 5 and White a 6. White having thrown the higher number has the first move and must play 6:5. White now has a choice; he can move one man for 6 points, and another man for 5 points; or alternatively he can move one man for the full 11 points. Bear in mind that when you move one man for the total of the two dice you actually make 2 moves with the same man, and you must touch down on a point between moves. You do not jump all 11 points in one move. *Diagram 4* shows how White moves one man for 11 points. In this case he decides to move a runner from Black's 1 point. He starts the count from the point adjacent to the one on

DIAGRAM 5

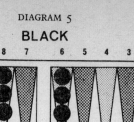

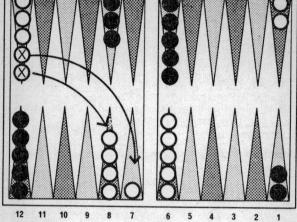

DIAGRAM 6

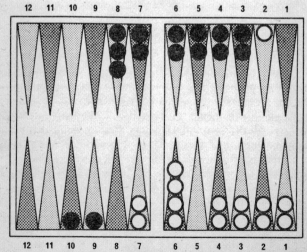

which he stands, and in moving passes over and counts every point on the way, whether they have men on them or not. The bar does not count as a point; it simply serves to divide the board into the inner and outer boards. A move of 6 brings White's runner to the opponent's bar point (B7), where for a moment he touches down, and then moves on a further 5 points to join his five men on B12. There is no limit to the number of men of one colour that may be placed upon a point. The alternative choice for White is to move two different men, one for 5 points and the other for 6 points. *Diagram 5* shows White moving one man B12–W8, and the other B12–W7.

Blocked points

When a player has two or more men on a point he 'owns' that point, and an opponent cannot land on it, nor may he touch down on it when moving the combined total of two dice. Look again at *diagram 4* and you will see that White cannot move 5:6. If he tries to move the 5 first he finds that he must touch down on B6 which is 'owned' or occupied by Black. By moving the 6 before the 5 he can arrange the move so that he touches down on a vacant point (B7) and then moves on another 5 points to reach the safety of a point owned by him. A player who positions 2 or more men on a point is said to have 'made a point'.

A prime

A player who makes 6 consecutive points has completed a 'prime'. An opposing man trapped behind a prime cannot move past, for it cannot be moved more than six spaces at a time, the largest number on the die. *Diagram 6* shows Black in this happy position with one of White's runners trapped behind his prime and unable to escape.

Blots

A single man on a point is called a 'blot'. In *diagram 7* White has a 'blot' on W7 after he has completed his move. If Black can

DIAGRAM 7

BLACK

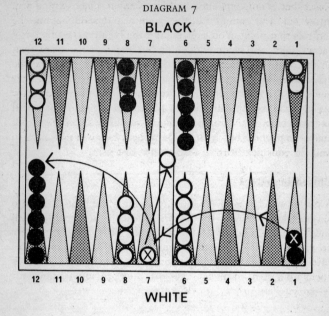

WHITE

move a man onto W7, or touch down on it whilst moving the combined total of 2 dice, the blot is hit, is removed from the board and placed upon the bar. In *diagram 7* Black throws 6:5, and promptly decides to move one runner the whole way touching down on White's blot on W7 on the way and sending it to the bar, and continuing his move to the safety of a point he owns, W12.

Entering a man from the bar

When you have a man (or men) on the bar you are not permitted to make any move until it (or they) get back onto the board. The man on the bar must re-enter the game in the opponent's home board. To re-enter the man, you must first throw a number on either die that corresponds to a point in your opponent's home board that is not controlled by him. Thus in *diagram 7*, if you throw 6:4, you cannot re-enter your man on B6 because he controls that point. You can re-enter the man on B4 which is a vacant point, and having done this you may now move any man on the board with the 6. If you have two or more men on the bar, you must get them all in before you can make any other move. In *diagram 7*, if you had two men on the bar and throw 6:4 you could only enter one man on the 4 point. As you still have one man on the bar which could not be re-entered you are unable to play the 6, which would be lost. You will now have to wait for your next turn to re-enter the last man.

Closed board

A player who has made all 6 points in his home board is said to have a 'closed board'. In *diagram 8* Black has a closed board, and White has a man waiting for re-entry on the bar. There are no vacant points in Black's home board so White cannot re-enter, and he must forfeit his turns until such time as Black opens up a point in his home board, thus providing a point for re-entry.

Moving doubles

If the same number appears on both dice, *i.e.* 6:6 or 3:3, this is known as a 'doublet', and the player is entitled to 4 moves instead of 2. By throwing 6:6 he can make 4 moves, each of 6 points. In *diagram 9* White has thrown 6:6, and decides to move both his runners B1–B7, to make his opponent's bar point, and then to move two men B12–W7 to make his own bar point. This of course would be a very satisfactory start to the game for White. In one move he achieves two major tactical advantages. Firstly, his two runners have made a flying start on the journey home and in the process have captured one of his opponent's most important blockading points. Secondly, he has made excellent progress in blocking Black's two runners by closing up his own bar point, giving him the beginnings of a blockade based on the three points: W8, W7 and W6. The great advantage of all

DIAGRAM 8
BLACK

12 11 10 9 8 7 6 5 4 3 2 1

12 11 10 9 8 7 6 5 4 3 2 1

WHITE

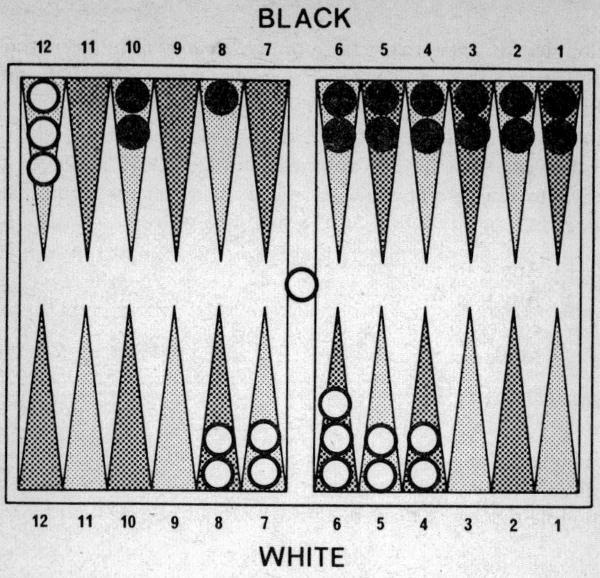

DIAGRAM 9
BLACK

12 11 10 9 8 7 6 5 4 3 2 1

12 11 10 9 8 7 6 5 4 3 2 1

WHITE

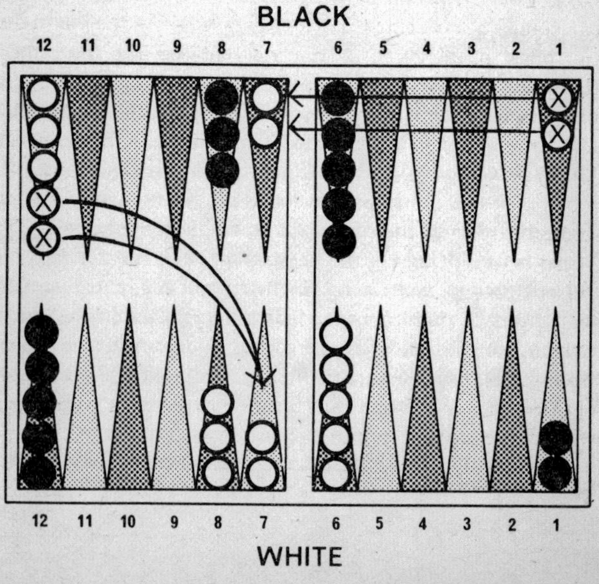

doublet throws is that you can move your men in pairs, thereby always making a point and never exposing a blot. You do not have to move in pairs however; you can elect to play the four moves of the double in any way you like.

For example, if you throw 2:2 you have 4 moves of 2 points each to make, and you can move them in any combination, *e.g.*:

1 Any four men for 2 points each;
2 Any two men for 2 points each, and any other man for two consecutive moves of 2 points;
3 Move one man 2 points, and another man for 3 consecutive moves of 2 points;
4 Move one man for 4 consecutive moves of 2 points.

Though you have complete freedom to use the 4 moves of a double in any combination you like, you will tend to use the double throws to make points by moving in pairs.

Bearing off

Once a player has brought all his men into his home board, he can commence bearing off. Men removed from the board during this phase of the game are never re-entered into the game, and the winner is the player who first removes all his men. A player may not bear off so long as he has a man on the bar, or outside his home board. If during the process of bearing off the player leaves a blot that is hit by his opponent, he cannot bear off any more men. First he must re-enter the blot in his opponent's home board, and then bring it round the board into his home board before resuming the bearing off process.

Look now at *diagram 10*. White throws 6:4, and removes one man from W6 and another from W4. Black throws double 6 (which like all doubles is played twice), and removes three men from B6. Then because he has no more men on B6, he is entitled to remove one man from B5, the next highest point, with the remaining move.

Diagrams 11 and 12 illustrate another aspect. Both White and

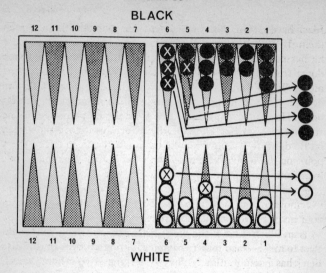

DIAGRAM 10

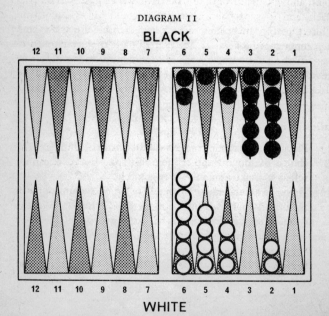

DIAGRAM 11

Black have gaps in their home boards, *i.e.* points with no men on them. If White throws a 3:1 he cannot remove any men because he has no men on those points. Instead he must move a man down from a higher point to a lower point. In *diagram 12* he moves W6–W3 and W2–W1. Black in the same diagram throws double 5. With the first 5 he removes the one man on the B5 point. He cannot remove any men from the B4 point because he still has men on B6. Therefore he is forced to move the 2 men on B6 down to B1. Now that he has no further men left on the 5 point or the 6 point, he must with his last move, remove one man from his 4 point.

When the bearing off stage is reached you are not compelled to remove a man. If it suits your purpose you may move within your home board instead of taking a man off the board. *Diagram 13* is an illustration of the type of situation in which you would elect to move a man rather than take it off the board. In this case Black has a man waiting on the bar to re-enter your home board, and White throws 6:5. If he now removes one man from the 6 point, and one man from the 5 point he will expose two blots to Black, and it is probable that Black would hit one of them. White therefore must first remove a man from W6 with the 6 (he cannot move a 6 within the home board so is compelled to bear off the man with the 6). The remaining man on W6 he moves 5 points W6–W1. In this way no blots are exposed for Black to hit.

Rules of movement

1   Plays must be made for both dice if possible. You have the choice of moving either number first, but you cannot refuse to make a move if it is possible.

2   If you can make one or other of your moves, but not both, then the higher one must be made. In *diagram 14* White is down to his last two men and Black is still waiting in your home board hoping to hit a blot. If you now throw 3:1, you would obviously like to play the one by moving a man from W5 to cover the blot on W4. If you do this you

DIAGRAM 12

BLACK

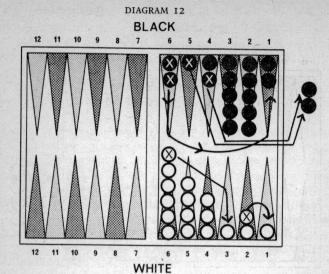

WHITE

DIAGRAM 13

BLACK

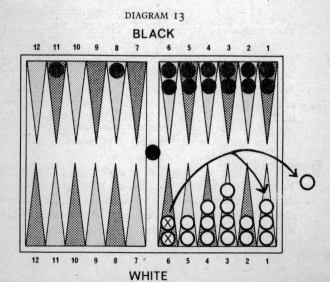

WHITE

DIAGRAM 14

BLACK

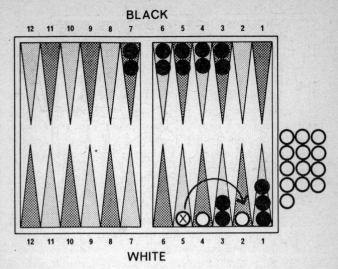

WHITE

would be unable to move the 3. The rule states that if both moves cannot be made, then the higher must be moved first. White is forced to make a compulsory move W5–W2. He cannot move the 1 which is forfeited and he finds that he is still forced to expose two blots to Black.

3   An incorrect move must be corrected before the subsequent throw of the opposing player. Once the opponent throws his dice previous moves (correct or incorrect) stand.

Throwing the dice

1   Each player throws his dice onto the board on his right.
2   As long as he leaves the dice on the board, the player may change his moves several times if he wishes. Picking up his dice is the signal that his move is completed, and once he picks up his dice he may not change his move.

3 If the opponent throws his dice before you have picked up your dice, he must pick them up and re-throw them after you have completed your turn. He may not use the dice that were thrown out of turn.

4 If a die jumps the bar, falls outside the right-hand board, lands flat on a man, or ends up in a tilted position, then both dice have to be re-thrown.

5 At the start of any game, either player may demand that the dice be mixed. To do this all four dice are placed in one cup, shaken and spilled out onto the board. Each player in turn then picks one die for his own use until all four have been selected. Mixing the dice is not done in the middle of a game.

Scoring

There are several methods of scoring in backgammon, but in this book we only use the traditional one. If you get all your men off the board before your opponent, you win a single game and score one point. If you 'gammon' your opponent by getting all your men off the board before he has removed a single man you win a double game and score 2 points. If you 'backgammon' your opponent, by getting all your men off the board whilst he still has a man on the bar, or in your home board, you win a triple game and score 3 points. The purpose of the double and triple game is to allow the winner to earn a suitable reward for a decisive victory.

The doubling cube

The doubling cube brings to backgammon extra excitement, tension and skill. Each face of the cube bears a number to record the progressive doubles and re-doubles, starting with 2 and goes on 4, 8, 16, 32 and 64. At the start of the game the doubling cube is placed in the centre of the bar, mid-way between the two players with the face turned to 64. This indicates that the cube is zero, and that neither player has possession of it. At any point during the game, a player who thinks he is in a winning position, may, when it is his turn to play, and before he casts his dice, double the stakes by turning the cube to 2, and pushing it towards his opponent's side of the board. His opponent has the choice of accepting (in which case the game continues at double the original stake) or refusing. If he declines a double the game is over, and he must pay over one unit of stake. The player who accepts the double draws the cube to his side of the board, and now 'owns' the cube. He now has the right to re-double his opponent at any point during the rest of the game, but the original doubler cannot re-double. If fortune favours him he can exercise his option to re-double his opponent, who will in turn be faced with the choice of refusing and paying up 2 units of stake, or accepting and playing for 4 units of stake. If he accepts he will then 'own' the cube, and only he can re-double the stake to 8, if he judges the situation to be in his favour.

When a player is on the bar, facing a closed board so that he cannot make a move, he still has the right to double his opponent should he wish to do so.

Scoring with doubles

If the cube is at 2, and you win, you collect 2 units of the starting stake. If you win by a gammon (or double game) the loser must pay twice the amount on the cube, *i.e.* $2 \times 2 = 4$ times the starting stake. Likewise if the cube is at 4, and you win by a backgammon the winnings are 3 times the amount on the cube, $3 \times 4 = 12$ times the starting stake.

Automatic doubles

Before playing backgammon you must settle with your opponent the question of automatic doubles. They take several different forms, the two most common ones being:

1   If, in throwing for the first move, doubles are thrown, the cube is automatically doubled. If this is followed by another double, then the cube is automatically turned to 4 and so on each time you throw a double for the opening

move. In this way the game can start with 2, 4, 8 or more times the original agreed stake.

2   In addition some players allow each player to refuse the first throw of the dice, and to double the cube to gain the right to re-cast the dice in the hope of obtaining a more favourable throw.

With all automatic doubles no one gains possession of the cube which remains in the middle of the board. If you are an inexperienced player and you are playing for money you would be well advised not to agree to automatic doubles, as it can cause sudden and enormous escalation of the stakes. You may have started out agreeing to play for £1 per point and then, to your horror, find that after three automatic doubles, one double during the game and a loss involving a gammon, you have lost £32.

It is far safer to play for a higher starting stake than to agree to open-ended automatic doubles. There are other forms of automatic doubles, and re-doubles not discussed here, so take care to establish the position clearly before you start to play.

2 Basic Strategy

The opening move; response to the opening move

Having the opening move is an advantage as you have the opportunity to dictate the strategy of the game instead of merely reacting to your opponent. Start the game with two basic objects in mind.

1 To try and trap your opponent's runners behind a blockade.
2 To escape with your two runners before he can trap you.

Set your backgammon board up in front of you, move and study each move on your board as it is discussed. All moves in this chapter are for White.

At the end of this book there is a table of opening moves suitable for comparatively inexperienced players, and we will now examine some of them and the strategy behind them. The first player always plays the two dice thrown for the opening move, so he can never start with a double. The opening moves can be grouped as follows:

1 Aggressive (Those moves designed to trap the opponent's runners):
   A The point-making throws.
   B The 5-point builders.
   C The outer board builders.

2 Defensive (Those moves designed to escape with your runners):
   A Plain running moves.
   B Mixed run/block moves.

The point-making moves

There are 5 opening point-making throws, 3 of which are so outstanding that no one ever does anything else. These three are:

6:1   White moves B12–W7, W8–W7 to make this bar point (*diagram 15*).

3:1   White moves W8–W5, W6–W5 to make his 5 point (*diagram 16*).

4:2   White moves W8–W4, W6–W4 to make his 4 point (*diagram 17*).

In each of these cases White is starting a process of building a blockade and hopes to add to it on his future turns until he can trap one or two of the black runners behind a 6-point prime.

DIAGRAM 15

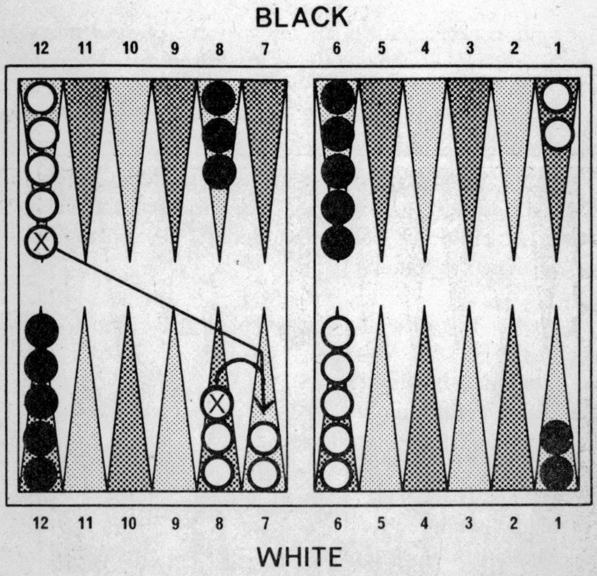

BLACK

WHITE

DIAGRAM 16

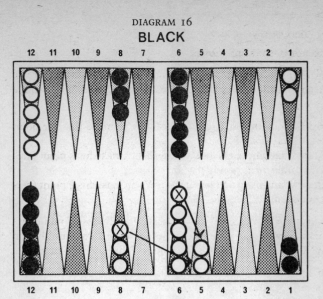

DIAGRAM 17

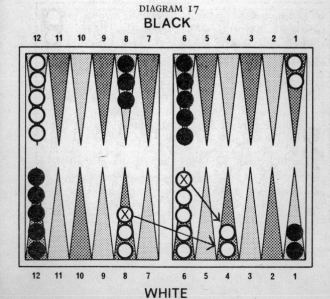

There are two other point-making opening throws which you should try out on your board:

5:3   White moves W8–W3, W6–W3 to gain control of his 3 point.

6:4   White moves W8–W2, W6–W2 to gain control of his 2 point.

These two moves are rarely played by any experienced player. Their only attraction is that they are safe point-making throws. The two men situated on either the 2 or 3 point are too far away from the main blockade which you must build round your 6 and 8 points, and Black can jump them both only too easily when he wants to escape with his runners. By positioning two men on the 2 or 3 point they are no real threat to Black, and in effect two men that are needed to build a blockade further back are wasted in a position where they make little contribution to the game in its early stages.

The 5-point builders

This group, unlike the safe point-making throws, involves you in taking a risk by leaving a blot on your 5 point, and hoping that Black will not hit it, thus giving you a chance to cover it on your next turn, to gain control of your vital 5 point.

5:3 *or* 6:2   Move a man B12–W5 (*diagram 18*).

2:1, 4:1, *or* 5:1   In each case you move the one by dropping a blot onto the 5 point, and bring down a builder onto your outer board, to increase the chances of covering it at the next turn.

Diagram 19 shows the 2:1 move; try out the other two yourself. Leaving a blot on your 5 point may look very exposed, but in actual fact, of the 36 permutations of the dice, only 15 of them will enable Black to hit your blot on the 5 point. However, 6 of those 15 permutations are his own vital point-making throws, such as 1:1, 2:2, 3:1, 4:2, *etc.* He will therefore be faced with the agonising choice, break up your budding blockade, or make his

DIAGRAM 18

BLACK

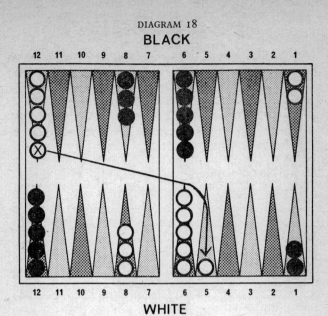

WHITE

DIAGRAM 19

BLACK

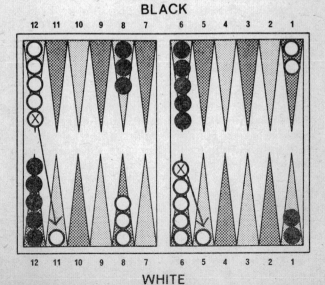

WHITE

own? At this stage of the game when Black has 5 points open in his home board, being hit, though annoying, is not dangerous. You will quickly be able to re-enter his board. It is very important to take your risks at the beginning of the game whilst Black's home board is open, but do not take risks later in the game when his board is almost closed, and re-entry can cause great difficulty.

The outer board builders

This group of opening moves requires you to bring down two builders from B12 and leave two blots on your outer board, with the intention of enhancing your chances of making W9, W7, W5 or W4 on your next turn. At such a distance Black can only hit you with a very above-average throw, so with his board wide open the risk is well worth while. You would make such a move if your opening throw was 5:2, 5:3, 4:3, 3:2.

Diagram 20 illustrates the 4:3 move. White moves B12–W9, B12–W10. Try out the other moves on your own board, moving as follows:

5:2	B12–W8, B12–W11		6:4	B12–W7, B12–W9
5:3	B12–W8, B12–W10		6:3	B12–W7, B12–W10
5:4	B12–W8, B12–W9		6:2	B12–W7, B12–W11
3:2	B12–W10, B12–W11			

Running opening moves

If run and escape is to be your policy, rather than to try and trap Black, you would run with the following moves: 6:5, 6:4, 6:3, 6:2, 5:4 and 5:3. All are good running moves enabling you to get a runner well out onto Black's outer board. In *diagram 21* with a throw of 6:2 White runs B1–B9. Try out the other outer board running combinations on your own board. Black will frequently miss the blot and many moves which enable him to hit it entail wasting a vital point-making move. So by running to the outer board you do have a reasonable chance of escaping. The smaller throws such as 3:2, 4:3, 2:1, can also be used as running throws. In *diagram 22* the 4:3 move is played B1–B5, B1–B4.

DIAGRAM 20

BLACK

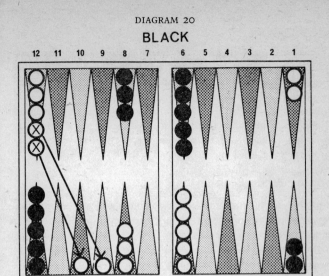

WHITE

DIAGRAM 21

BLACK

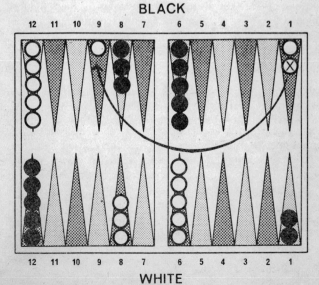

WHITE

This is an annoying move for Black. Firstly, you are threatening to escape with your two runners. Secondly, he will hesitate to leave a blot anywhere on his outer board, or on his 5 point, as the chances of a hit are now greatly enhanced. Thirdly, you are threatening to capture one of his vital points, such as the 5 point or the bar point, on your next turn. Much the same applies to the other inner board running moves. Try them out playing 3:2   B1–B3, B1–B4 and 2:1   B1–B3, B1–B2.

Mixed run/block openers

This type of opening move requires one runner to start a running move in the opponent's home board, and the dropping of a blot onto the player's outer board, to enhance the chances of making one of the blocking points on the next turn. In *diagram 23* you see how White uses 4:3 by playing B1–B5, B12–W10. An opening move of this sort makes it difficult for Black to play his normal tactics. Firstly, by placing a man on B5 you are threatening to cover it from B1 on your next turn, and to gain control of a point vital to Black. Secondly, the man on B5 makes it difficult for Black to drop a blot onto his outer board. Thirdly, your blot on W10 equally makes it dangerous for Black to move a blot to W4, W5, W7 and W9. This mixed run/block type of opener can be done with many dice combinations, 5:4, 3:2, 2:1, *etc.* They all reduce the options open to Black when he responds to the opening move.

Responses to the opening move

As the responder you do not have as much freedom of action as the opener. By his choice of opening move he reduces the choices open to you. However, the one compensation is that you could throw a double, and all doubles are nice safe point-making throws. Therefore we start by examining all the doubles that might come your way and how to play them.

In *diagram 24* Black has opened 3:2 and played W12–B10, W1–W3. You get 6:6. You move two men B1–B7 and the other two men B12–W7, a perfect response with your runners well on

DIAGRAM 22

BLACK

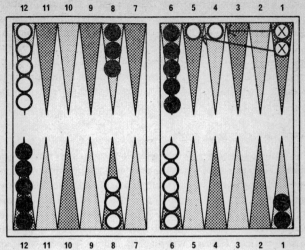

WHITE

DIAGRAM 23

BLACK

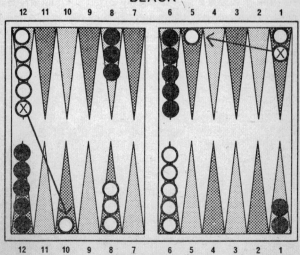

WHITE

the way to escaping and at the same time you have blocked off the 7 point to create a 3-point blockade in front of Black's escape route. Some players always double when they throw a double 6 for the response. If this is ever done to you, accept. It may be a flying start, but there are difficulties ahead for the double 6 player; his men are now clustered together in a way that makes it difficult for him not to expose a blot with future moves.

In *diagram 25* you get 5:5. Of all the doubles, this is the worst one to get at the beginning of a game. There is normally only one way to play this move: you play two men B12–W8, and the same two men W8–W3 to make the 3 point. However, in this instance Black has split his back men on the opening move and turned what is normally a poor throw into a crushing blow. Your correct play is to move two men from W8 to hit Black's blot on W3 and two men W6–W1 to hit his second blot on W1. Two of Black's men off the board in one throw, and you have closed three of the re-entry points at the same time. If Black fails to get his two men re-entered on his next throw you should instantly double him, and if he is wise he will refuse your double and pay up, as his position is very adverse.

If your throw is double 4, you have many choices open to you. If your policy is to run, then move your two runners B1–B5 and on again B5–B9, *diagram 26*. If your choice is to block Black's runners then you would move B12–W9 and the same men on again W9–W5 to make your 5 point, *diagram 27*. If you wish to play a mixed run/block game then play two men B1–B5, and two men B12–W9. Try all these moves on your own board.

If your throw is double 3, you have another perfect throw. If run is your policy you would move your two runners to the black bar point, B7. This however would be a waste for a double 3 which is one of the best blockading doubles. If Black has not split his back men you would play two men B12–W10, and two men W8–W5, as in *diagram 28*. However, when Black has split his runners, your blot on W8 would be too vulnerable to risk this move. Far better in these circumstances to play W6–W3 to hit his blot, and W8–W5 both to make your vital 5 point and to reduce his chances of re-entry (*diagram 29*). A sharp reverse for

DIAGRAM 24

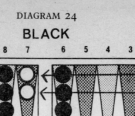

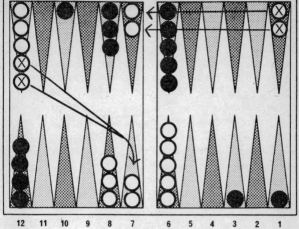

DIAGRAM 25

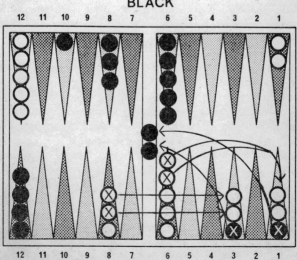

DIAGRAM 26

BLACK

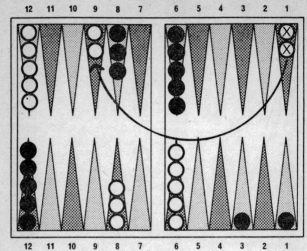

WHITE

DIAGRAM 27

BLACK

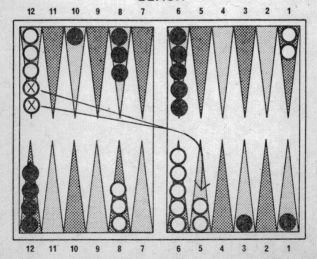

WHITE

DIAGRAM 28

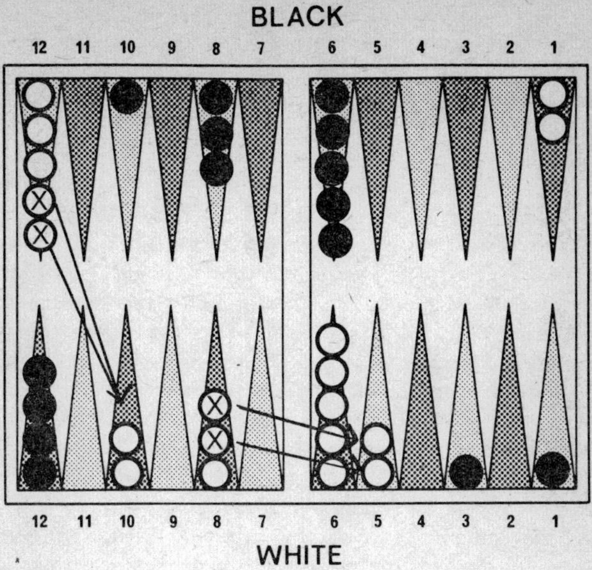

BLACK

WHITE

DIAGRAM 29

BLACK

WHITE

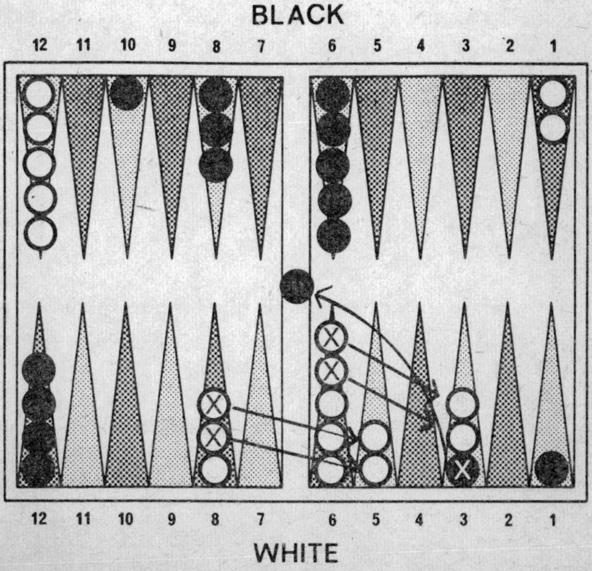

Black, but not quite good enough for you to double him. At this stage of the game you would only double him if you have knocked two of his men off the board as occurred in diagram 25 with your double 5.

If your throw is double 2, you again have a throw that is too valuable to waste on running with your runners. You could use it to make your 9 point moving two men B12–W9, but it is probably best to move as in *diagram 30* to make your 4 point, two men W6–W4, and two men to your 11 point, B12–W11.

If your throw is double 1, there are only two moves worth considering. If Black has not split his back men you play two men W8–W7, and two men W6–W5 to gain control of the three most important points, *diagram 31*. If, however, Black has split his back runners as in *diagram 32*, your blot on W8 is too vulnerable to a return shot from Black, so you play the double 1 by moving W8–W5 with one man, and the remaining one is played W6–W5 to cover the 5 point.

At the end of this book you will find listed 29 different choices for the opening moves. To each of these 29 opening moves there are at least 30 different responses, making a total of 870 possible ways of playing. Therefore it is obvious that in a book of this size there is only space to discuss the principles by which you select your response to the opening move, which are as follows:

1   If your opponent's move does not make it adverse, play your moves as though you were the opener.

2   With rare exceptions, play all important point-making throws to make the important points, in order to trap your opponent's runners, *i.e.* 1:1, 2:2, 3:3, 4:4, 6:6, 3:1, 4:2 and 6:1.

3   If your opponent has split his runners but still has both of them in your inner board the risk of dropping a blot onto W5 or W7 to try and make a vital point is too great: it will almost certainly be hit.

4   If your opponent is threatening either to escape or gain control of your vital 4, 5 and 7 points by placing a blot on

DIAGRAM 30

BLACK

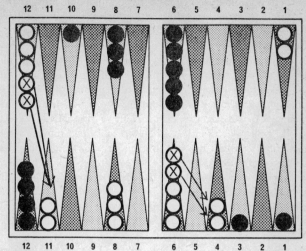

WHITE

DIAGRAM 31

BLACK

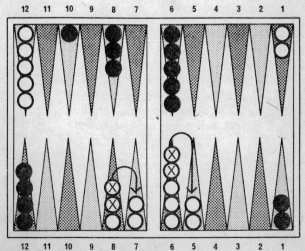

WHITE

DIAGRAM 32
BLACK

WHITE

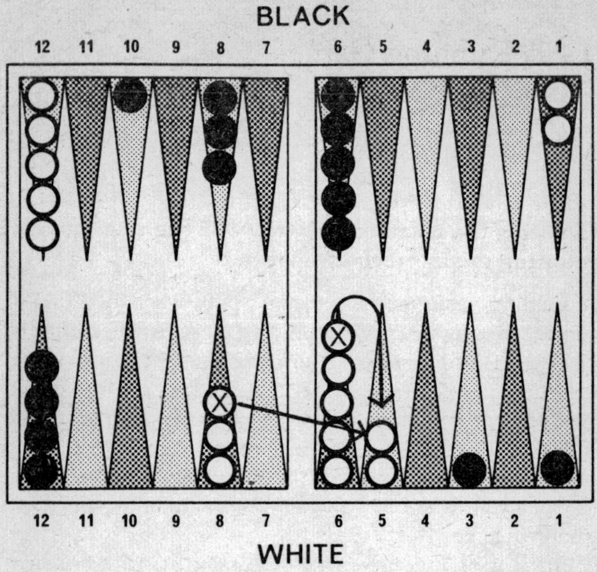

them, give serious consideration to hitting him and driving him back.

5 Do not bother to hit his blots on your 1, 2 or 3 points; there will normally be better ways of playing your move at this stage of the game.

6 If he has moved into his inner or outer board, threatening to try and block in your runners, hit him and break up the blockade before it can form, but not at the expense of making your 5 or 7 point.

7 If there is nothing constructive to do with your throw and you can hit two of your opponent's men in one move, do so, even if it means that you might have to leave a blot in your home board.

8 If you are forced to leave a blot in a vulnerable situation, select a position where, if it is not hit, it will enable you to gain a vital point if you can cover it on your next turn.

3   A Running Game

Counting the position; the tricks of running movements; counting the number of turns left.

A running game normally occurs only when both sides have succeeded early in advancing their runners to safe outposts. The chances of hitting blots, or of blocking enemy men have been considerably reduced as a result. A running game is the only type of game where the dice have a decisive say in the outcome. The player getting the higher numbers (provided he makes no movement errors) is normally the winner.

Open your board, set up your men, and follow this illustrative running game.

Black wins the opening move and plays 3:1 to make his 5 point, with the intention of building up a blockade, *diagram 33*. White throws 6:5 and promptly runs with his runner B1–B12 to produce the situation in *diagram 34*.

Black now throws 5:1 and plays W12–B8, B6–B5 (*diagram 35*). Note how Black has a spare man positioned on each point, B8, B6 and B5. This gives him a very high probability of making yet another blocking point on his next turn. 6:1 would make the bar point, and he would make the 4 point with 4:1, 4:2 or 2:1, *etc*. From White's viewpoint the position has deteriorated: he has made no progress in building a blockade, and his remaining runner is rapidly being hemmed into Black's home board. White throws and gets 6:3 and in view of the threatening shape of Black's board decides to run, moving B1–B10 (*diagram 36*). Very annoying for Black; his promising blockade is quite useless unless he can hit a white blot and force it back into his home board, so mentally praying for a 3 he throws his dice and gets 6:6 and makes

DIAGRAM 33

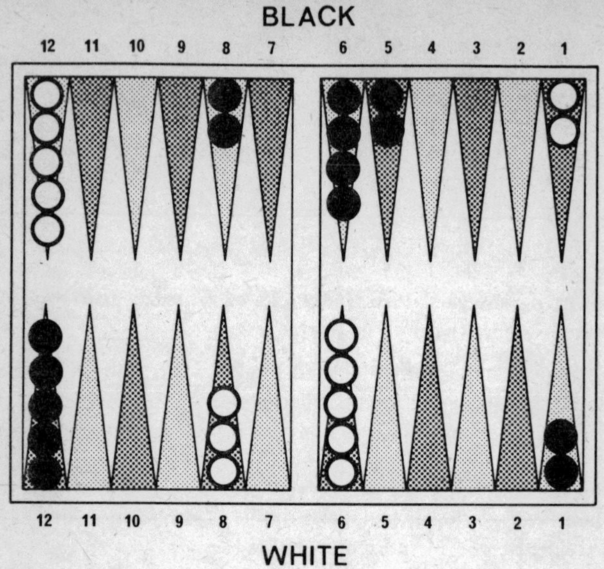

BLACK

WHITE

DIAGRAM 34

BLACK

WHITE

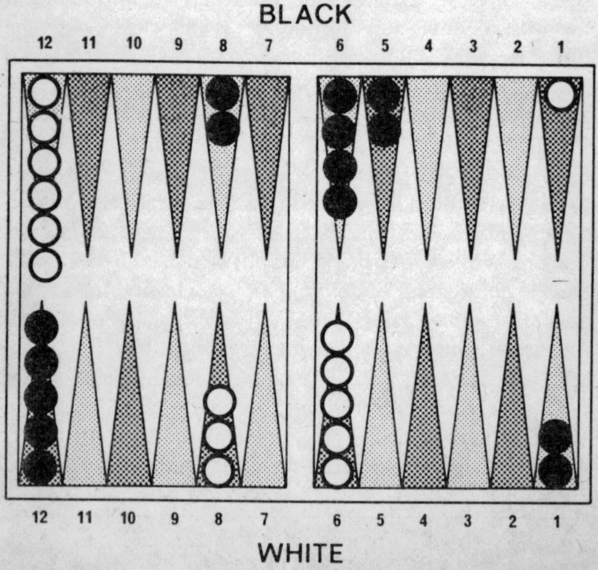

DIAGRAM 35

BLACK

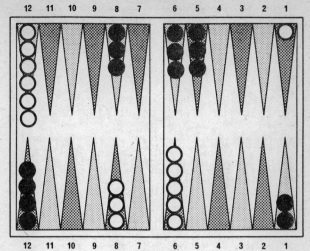

WHITE

DIAGRAM 36

BLACK

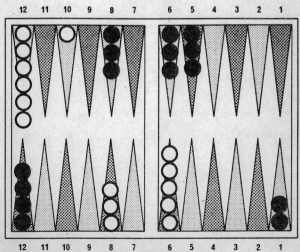

WHITE

DIAGRAM 37

BLACK

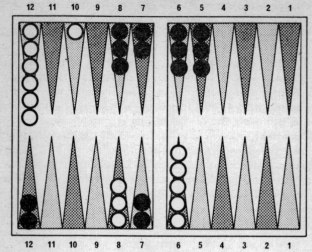

WHITE

DIAGRAM 38

BLACK

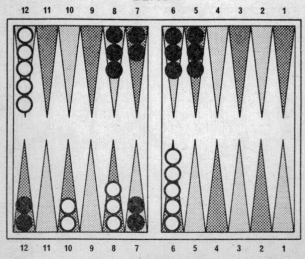

WHITE

the classic move, two men W1–W7 and two men W12–B7 to make both bar points, thus producing the situation in *diagram 37*.

For White the situation is not good. His blot on B10 has survived, but the chances of getting it to safety are not very good; if Black hits it on the next turn he would be in a position either to double White, or possibly even to gammon him. White realises that his only hope is to play a safe running game, throws his dice and gets 5:3. With a sigh of relief he makes his 10 point, moving B10–W10, B12–W10 (*diagram 38*).

This will provide a very badly needed safe landing-point for the men coming home from the B12 point.

Black now throws 2:1 and moves B6–B4, B5–B4 to make his 4 point (*diagram 39*). White also throws 2:1 and plays B12–W10 to produce the situation in *diagram 40*.

Black surveying the scene realises that the chances of hitting a

DIAGRAM 39

BLACK

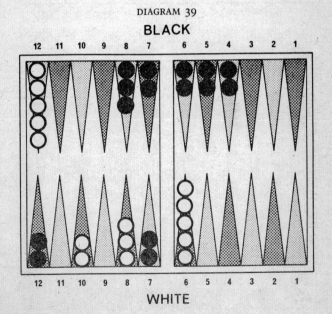

WHITE

white blot have almost gone, and his superb blockade is now virtually useless to him, so there is no longer any great advantage in leaving his two runners on W7. It is not easy for Black to run for home, and the difficulty is to get his two men on W7 clear without exposing a shot to White. Undecided, he throws his dice and gets double 4. Now he must decide, run or stay in the hope of a shot at White? Sometimes it is quite obviously simple to make such a decision when one side is clearly in the lead, but in *diagram 40* it is by no means clear who *is* in the lead, so Black decides to make an accurate count of the position.

Counting the position

For a moment we break off the running game and explain how to count the position. The count represents the number of points you would have to move (assuming no wasted motion), to

DIAGRAM 40

BLACK

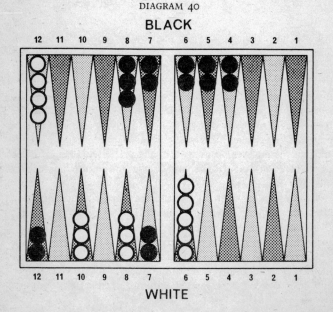

WHITE

move your men into the home board and bear them all off. The count of each man in your home and outer boards is that of the point he is on. A man on your 6 point counts 6, a man on your 8 point counts 8, *etc*. The count for your men on your opponent's board starts at 13 for his 12 point, 14 for his 11 point, and so on to 24 for his 1 point. Look at *diagram 40* and count the position for both Black and White.

Black's count					White's count				
2 men on B4	= 2 × 4	= 8							
2 men on B5	= 2 × 5	= 10							
2 men on B6	= 2 × 6	= 12		5 men on W6	= 5 × 6	= 30			
2 men on B7	= 2 × 7	= 14		3 men on W8	= 3 × 8	= 24			
3 men on B8	= 3 × 8	= 24		3 men on W10	= 3 × 10	= 30			
2 men on W12	= 2 × 13	= 26		4 men on B12	= 4 × 13	= 52			
2 men on W7	= 2 × 18	= 36							
Total		130			*Total*		136		

Black finds that he is in the lead by 6 points, or about 5%. This is not much of a lead, as he would normally like to see an 8 to 10% lead before deciding to make a run for it. However in this case there is not much alternative; if he stays there is little likelihood of White exposing a blot. If Black now deducts the value of his current throw from his count, he finds that after he has made his move his count will be 114, giving him a lead of 22 points. The average throw of the dice is $8\frac{1}{6}$ (after making allowance for the doubles) so that a lead of 22 represents almost three turns. He hesitates no longer and decides to run, moving his two men W7–B10 (*diagram 41*).

White, who has virtually been forced to play a running game after his opening move, now finds that he is falling behind Black, and worse still, if he does not throw big dice on his next turn he can expect Black to double him.

Again we must pause in the running game to examine the best method of movement in the running game stage. Most games end up in a race for the home board once contact is broken off,

DIAGRAM 41

BLACK

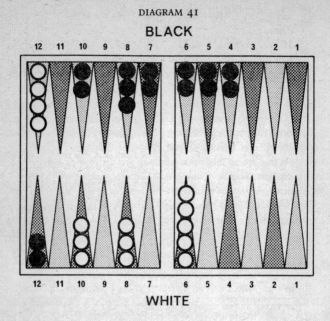

WHITE

and it is vital to be familiar with the correct methods of movement in this situation.

Running game movement

1   Every move must be utilised to its utmost, do not waste a single point. Your first objective is to get all your men into your home board as fast as possible. You aim to get them on your 6 point. This may well give you a very bad distribution with a huge pile on the 6 point, but by doing this you will find that you start getting the first man off the board quicker than if you used the points to move them further into the home board.

2   High throws should NOT be used to move men from your outer board to low points in your home board if you still

have men further away. Use them to bring in the most distant men.

3 If you still have men on your opponent's outer board, bring them down to your outer board first, where they are within reach of your home board with the throw of one die, rather than requiring two dice to get them in.

4 If possible each move should make a man change boards (*i.e.* from your opponent's outer board to your outer board, or from your outer board to your inner board) and should not be used to move within the same board.

5 As you move into your home board try and place your men on open points (so long as it does not waste a part of your move) to help you bear off one man with each die you throw.

6 When all your men are in the home board (no matter how badly distributed), remove a man if it is possible rather than move within the board.

DIAGRAM 42

BLACK

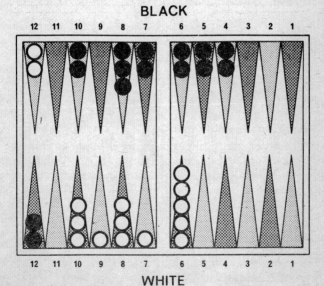

WHITE

DIAGRAM 43

BLACK

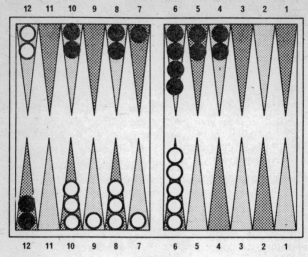

WHITE

DIAGRAM 44

BLACK

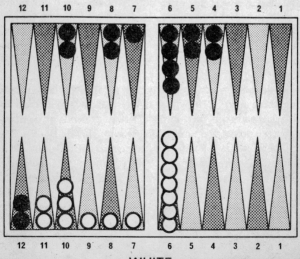

WHITE

Now we can resume the game. White throws 6:4, and plays B12–W7, B12–W9, *diagram 42*. The count is now Black, 114; White, 126. Black is in the lead by 12 points, and it is his turn to play next. A 10% lead in a running game is sufficient for a double, so before throwing his dice Black doubles White. So long as White is not more than 15% behind he should accept the double. The game proceeds and Black throws 2:1 (now he wishes he had not doubled!) But for White's two men on B12 he would use this throw to bring his two men on W12 down to his outer board, so in this case he plays B7–B6, B8–B6. Note that he does not waste a single point: both men change boards, and he moves men that exactly reach his 6 point. This produces the situation in *diagram 43*.

White now throws 2:2. He changes boards with his two most distant men, moving two men B12–W11, and moves two men W8–W6, so that not a point is wasted (*diagram 44*). Black in his turn throws 6:4 and brings down the two last men from W12 to B7 and B9 to produce the situation in *diagram 45*.

White throws 6:5 and correctly brings in his two most distant men moving W11–W5, W11–W6 (*diagram 46*). Black throws 6:5, and here he makes an error. The correct play would be to bring in his two most distant men, moving B10–B4, B10–B5. Instead he decides to fill in vacant points on his home board (desirable, but this should not be done at the expense of moving his two most distant men) and plays B9–B3, and B7–B2 to produce the situation in *diagram 47*. Black has wasted points that may well cost him the game if his next two throws are low ones.

White throws 5:5, and correctly moves his most distant men, playing three men W10–W5, and one man W9–W4 (*diagram 48*). Black throws 3:2, and, in his desire not to collect too many men on his 6 point, again makes an error by moving B8–B5, B7–B5. His correct play is to move both men on B8 to B5 and B6 to get minimum waste movement. This produces the situation in *diagram 49*.

White now throws 6:5, avoids the error of moving both men onto W2 and instead fills in two vacant points by playing

DIAGRAM 45

BLACK

| 12 | 11 | 10 | 9 | 8 | 7 | 6 | 5 | 4 | 3 | 2 | 1 |

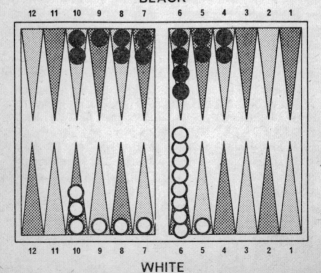

| 12 | 11 | 10 | 9 | 8 | 7 | 6 | 5 | 4 | 3 | 2 | 1 |

WHITE

DIAGRAM 46

BLACK

| 12 | 11 | 10 | 9 | 8 | 7 | 6 | 5 | 4 | 3 | 2 | 1 |

| 12 | 11 | 10 | 9 | 8 | 7 | 6 | 5 | 4 | 3 | 2 | 1 |

WHITE

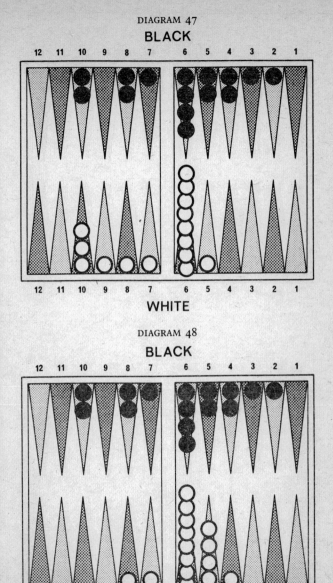

DIAGRAM 47

BLACK

12 11 10 9 8 7 6 5 4 3 2 1

WHITE

DIAGRAM 48

BLACK

12 11 10 9 8 7 6 5 4 3 2 1

WHITE

DIAGRAM 49

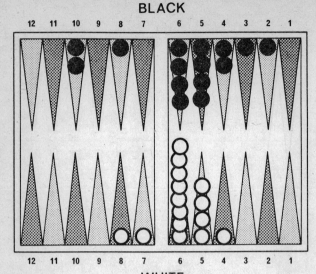

DIAGRAM 50

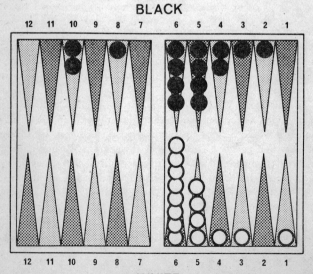

DIAGRAM 51

BLACK

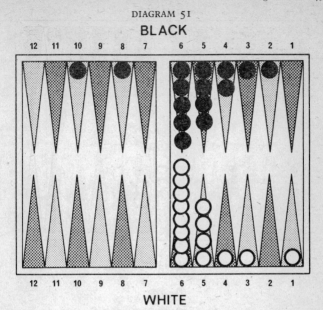

WHITE

W7–W1, W8–W3 (*diagram 50*). Black throws 3:1. Now his errors have caught him out. Instead of getting two men into his home board he can only move one man in, and this time correctly moves the most distant man B10–B6 to produce the situation in *diagram 51*.

At this stage White contemplates a re-double, but decides that in view of the fact that he has so many men on his 6 and 5 points it would be wise to wait another turn or two. He throws his dice and gets 3:1. He removes a man from W1 and another from W3, which still leaves him with all his men piled on his high points. Black throws a 6:1 and again can only get one man into his home board, moving B10–B4, B8–B7. (It is no good Black swearing about his unlucky dice. He has twice made errors of movement and as a result he still has one man outside his board; whereas if he had moved correctly he would now be in a

DIAGRAM 52

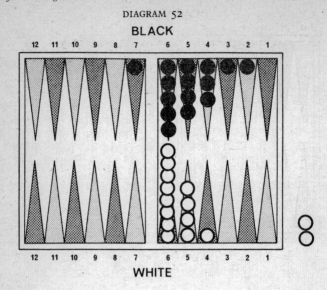

position virtually equal to White.) *Diagram 52* shows the position after these two moves.

In view of the bad distribution in his home board, White still hesitates to double, throws his dice and gets 4:4. He removes one man from W4, moves one man W5–W1 to fill the 1 point, and takes two men from W6 down to W2 to improve the distribution in his home board. Black throws 4:1, moves the last man B7–B6 and removes one man from B4 (*diagram 53*).

White throws 6:3, removes one man from his 6 point and another down W6–W3. Black throws 6:1, removes a man from his 6 point and plays the one by moving B5–B4 (*diagram 54*).

Counting the number of turns left

Again we must halt the game a moment and discuss judgement of the position during the end game. At this stage the point count method of judging the position ceases to have any use. If

DIAGRAM 53

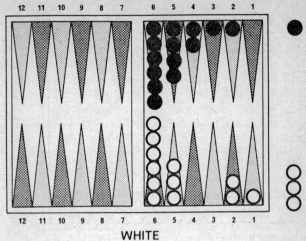

DIAGRAM 54

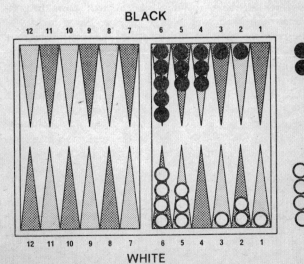

for example Black had only one man left on B6 his point count would be 6. If White had five men left on his 1 point his point count would be only 5. Excluding a lucky double it is going to take White three turns to remove all his men from the board (two with each throw of the dice), whereas Black is bound to remove his remaining man in two throws or less. Therefore in the end game it is not points that count, but rather the number of turns required to remove all your men from the board, assuming two men off with each throw of the dice.

Look now at *diagram 54*. White has four men off the board, and Black has two men off, leaving White with eleven men on the board and Black with thirteen. White would need $5\frac{1}{2}$ turns to get off, Black $6\frac{1}{2}$. Had he been 2 turns ahead White would have doubled instantly, but with the gaps in the middle of the board he decides to await the outcome of the next throw.

White throws 6:1, and removes men from the 6 and 1 points. Black throws 5:1, he moves one man from the 6 point to the one point and then takes the same man off the board. White now has nine men left on the board, Black has 12.

After the next throw of the dice White will, with a little luck, be four men ahead of Black, so he now offers Black a re-double to 4, to force him to retire. White, being ahead, does not want to risk Black throwing some high doubles to catch up. Black refuses the double. In this sort of situation you do not accept doubles where you must throw a high double to win. The odds are too much against you. With Black refusing the double the game comes to an end.

4 Luck, Odds, Chances, Probabilities

The simple arithmetic of backgammon

To play and win at backgammon you must understand *probability* (*i.e.* the likelihood that a given event will occur). This is the principle on which much business activity is based. Insurance companies work on the probability of an event occurring, not on luck. So too with backgammon. If you put your trust in that fickle mistress, 'luck', she will let you down.

Luck is of importance at any given moment. The novice can defeat the expert for one game if he has enough *'lucky'* dice. Everyone has the odd lucky throw, getting the one combination that can save the situation. At rubber bridge the novice, by holding all the big cards, can win a game, but over a series of games the luck of the deal in cards, or the dice in backgammon, evens out, and the skill of the expert bridge or backgammon player will show.

Even when luck is an important factor, you still need skill to make proper use of it. Probability is a science which, when correctly used in backgammon, is of the greatest help. Probability determines the odds of an event occurring, and you must be able to select the right move so that the probabilities of covering a blot, or the odds of being hit are as much in your favour as possible.

The 36 possibilities

There are 6 numbers on a die, and if you throw that die 6 times the probability of getting each individual number to turn up is 1 in 6. If however you throw it 1000 times the law of large numbers will apply and each number will turn up more or less the same number of turns. You may win one or two games by relying on lucky dice, but play 1000 games and you will only come out on top if you play to the laws of probability. In backgammon each die can be thrown 6 ways, which when multiplied together produces 36 possibilities. Imagine that you have two dice; the following table shows all possible 36 permutations into which the dice can fall.

TABLE I

The 36 Possibilities

	•	••	•••	•• ••	••• ••	••• •••
•	1-1	1-2	1-3	1-4	1-5	1-6
••	2-1	2-2	2-3	2-4	2-5	2-6
•••	3-1	3-2	3-3	3-4	3-5	3-6
•• ••	4-1	4-2	4-3	4-4	4-5	4-6
••• ••	5-1	5-2	5-3	5-4	5-5	5-6
••• •••	6-1	6-2	6-3	6-4	6-5	6-6

From this table note:

1   That the probability of a specific double turning up is 1 in 36.

2 That all non-double permutations turn up twice in 36, *i.e.* 1:6, 6:1.

3 That the probability of any one specific number turning up on either die is 11 in 36, *i.e.* there are 11 permutations that produce the number 1.

4 Although there are 36 permutations of the dice, there are only 21 combinations; 6:5 and 5:6, though different permutations of the dice, bring the man moved to the same destination.

5 Do not make the mistake of thinking that because you have not thrown a specific number (such as a 6) for the last 10 turns, that the probability of throwing a 6 in the next few turns has increased. The dice are inanimate and have no memory. The chances of throwing a 6 always remain the same—11 in 36—regardless of whether you have thrown a 6 ten times in a row, or if you have not had a 6 for the last ten turns.

In Table 2 (page 56) we apply these dice combinations to the probabilities of blot hitting.

Study this table and note:

1 The most dangerous place to leave a blot is exactly 6 points away from your opponent. His chances of hitting you are 17 in 36.

2 If you must expose a blot, try and expose it to an indirect shot (*i.e.* a number requiring the combined total of both dice to hit it). The further away you expose a blot the better the chances of survival.

3 If your blot is exposed to a direct shot (*i.e.* a number that is less than seven) place it as close to your opponent as possible. The chances of being hit become less as you get closer.

Blots and the opening move

In *diagram 55* you will see a figure printed at the top of each point. These figures show the number of your opponent's dice combinations that can hit a white blot exposed on each point.

TABLE 2

Probabilities of Hitting a Blot (Assuming opponent holds no points between you and the blot)

DICE COMBINATIONS	\multicolumn{17}{c}{DISTANCE OF BLOT}

DICE COMBINATIONS	1	2	3	4	5	6	7	8	9	10	11	12	15	16	18	20	24
6:6						1						1			1		1
6:5, 5:6					2	2					2						
6:4, 4:6				2		2				2							
6:3, 3:6			2			2			2								
6:2, 2:6		2				2		2									
6:1, 1:6	2					2	2										
5:5					1					1			1			1	
5:4, 4:5				2	2				2								
5:3, 3:5			2		2			2									
5:2, 2:5		2			2		2										
5:1, 1:5	2				2	2											
4:4				1				1				1		1			
4:3, 3:4			2	2			2										
4:2, 2:4		2		2		2											
4:1, 1:4	2			2	2												
3:3			1			1			1			1					
3:2, 2:3		2	2		2												
3:1, 1:3	2		2	2													
2:2		1		1		1		1									
2:1, 1:2	2	2	2														
1:1	1	1	1	1													
	11	12	14	15	15	17	6	6	5	3	2	3	1	1	1	1	1

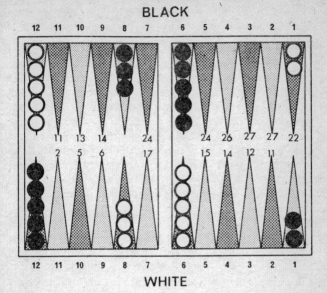

DIAGRAM 55

BLACK

WHITE

From this diagram you can quickly see that the 3 safest points on which to leave an opening move blot are W11, W10 and W9.

The strategic sacrifice

Diagram 55 reveals that one of the most dangerous points on which to leave a blot is B7. Twenty-four dice permutations can hit a blot exposed on that point. To a beginner it looks almost suicidal to move onto B7 with an opening move, a 66% chance that your opponent will hit you. Yet many of the most expert players use this as an opening move. Do not be put off by high chances of being hit, there is another reason for this move. If you do this there are:

19 chances in 36 that he can hit you, but is forced to leave a blot.

12 chances in 36 that he will miss your blot.
5 chances in 36 that he can hit you and cover his blot.
(*i.e.* 6:6, 3:3, 6:1, 1:6 and 1:1)

If he misses you (12 in 36) you will have 17 chances in 36 to
cover your blot from B1 on your next turn, and make your
opponent's important bar point. If he hits you and leaves a blot
(19 in 36) only 6:6 will stop you re-entering your man (1 in 36),
as his board is wide open. You will then have two separated men
in his inner board, giving you 22 chances in 36 of hitting his blot
on B7 with the second die. Although your blot was hit, and had
to go backwards some 4 or 5 points, his blot, when hit, has to go
back nearly 20 points to re-enter your home board, or over 2
average rolls of the dice. Many games of backgammon are won
by only one or two throws of the dice, so this is a major reverse
for your opponent.

Only 5 times in 36 will he hit and cover his blot to make the
bar point and your sacrifice will have been in vain. With all the
31 other permutations, the reward of hitting his blot, or of
making his bar point justify the risk taken. This sacrifice move
into B7 is particularly attractive if you have three men separated
in the opponent's home board. You would not do this move if
your opponent has made points in his inner board; you would
only do this as long as re-entry is easy, and should never risk
it if re-entry chances are reduced. Much the same argument
applies to B5, another of his vital points, and therefore a good
one on which to play an opening move.

TABLE 3

Probability of entering one or two men from the bar

Number of points open	Chances of coming in with 1 man	Chances of coming in with 2 men
5	97%	69%
4	89%	44%
3	75%	25%
2	56%	11%
1	31%	3%

DIAGRAM 56

BLACK

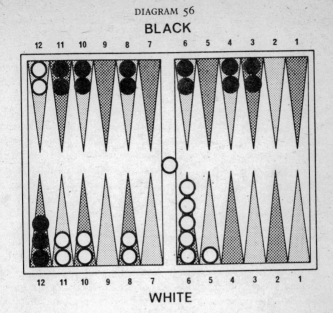

WHITE

To make this table quite clear look at *diagram 56*. Here is a situation where you have one man on the bar, and your opponent has 3 closed points and three open points. At first sight you might naturally think that the chances of re-entry are 50–50. In actual fact they are far better. Only 9 throws will stop re-entry (3:3, 4:4, 6:6, 6:3, 3:6, 6:4, 4:6, 4:3, 3:4). With the remaining 27 throws you will be able to re-enter your man, making the odds 3 to 1 or 75%.

Equally if you have two men on the bar your chances of re-entry will fall dramatically to a meagre 25%.

You must grasp clearly these probabilities of re-entry. Once your opponent starts to close up his board you must take great care never to give him the opportunity to get two of your men on the bar, and conversely it is worth paying almost any price to get two of his men on the bar.

TABLE 4

Probability of getting the last two men off the board in one or two throws of the dice

Pip points	Points on which located	Probabilities of getting off in one throw	Probability of getting off in two throws
12	6–6	11%	78%
11	6–5	17%	88%
10	5–5	17%	92%
	6–4	22%	93%
9	5–4	28%	96%
	6–3	28%	97%
8	4–4	31%	98%
	6–2	36%	99%
	5–3	39%	99%
7	6–1	42%	99%+
	4–3	47%	99%+
	5–2	53%	99%+
6	3–3	47%	100%
	5–1	64%	100%
	4–2	64%	100%
	6	75%	100%
5	3–2	69%	100%
	4–1	81%	100%
	5	86%	100%
4	2–2	72%	100%
	3–1	94%	100%
	4	94%	100%
3	2–1	100%	100%
	3	100%	100%
2	1–1	100%	100%
	2	100%	100%

Table 4 is used in end play situations. In *diagram 57* White throws a 6:1. He removes the man on W5 with the 6; but what is he to do with the 1? He can either move W4–W3, to place two men on W3, or he can move W3–W2. Which is correct? By

DIAGRAM 57

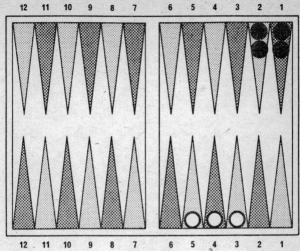

DIAGRAM 58

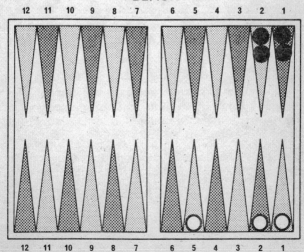

looking at Table 5 you will see that two men on W3 have a 47%
chance of being removed with the next throw of the dice, but if
the two men are split W4–W2 the chances rise to 64%.

In *diagram 58* White throws 2:1. He has three choices in front
of him.

1   Remove the man on W1, and move W5–W3, leaving a
    man on the W2 and a man on W3.
2   Remove a man on W2 and move W5–W4, leaving a man
    on W4 and the other on W1.
3   Remove 2 men from the W2 and W1 points, leaving
    one man on W5. Which is correct? Now look at Table 5 and
    you will find that if he does No. 1 (3–2) he has a 69%
    chance of getting off in one throw. With No. 2 (4–1) an
    81% chance. With No. 3, an 86% chance.

It is not necessary to memorise Table 4, though the more
familiar you are with it the better, but remember 3 basic facts
about end play:

1   Leave one man on a higher point, rather than 2 split men
    on lower points.
2   If you have two men left, and a move to make within your
    home board, move the lower man further down, rather
    than moving the higher one down.
3   Try and avoid leaving two men on the same point. If you
    have a choice keep them separate.

The arithmetic of the double

Common sense would seem to indicate that if an opponent is in
a position to double you, then conversely you must be in a
position where you must refuse the double. This is not correct;
there are many situations where it is both right to double, and
right to accept.

Diagram 59 is just such a situation. It is Black's turn to throw.
He knows that he has a 64% chance of removing both men on
the next throw (see Table 4) so he doubles White. White correctly accepts the double. Why? To make it clear, let us assume

DIAGRAM 59

BLACK

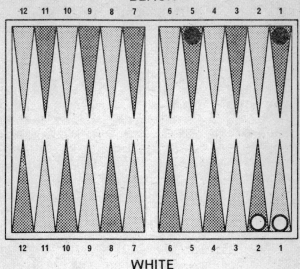

WHITE

that White found himself in this position 100 times in succession, and that he was playing for £1 per point. If, each time he was doubled he refused, he would pay over 100 × £1 = £100. However, if each time he was doubled he accepted the double, the result would be:

> *Lose* 64 times (doubled) 64 × £2 = £128
> *Win* 36 times (doubled) 36 × £2 = £ 72
> ———
> Result (*loss*)   £ 56

He still loses over the 100 games, but by accepting the double he reduces his loss from £100 to only £56. The break-even point for accepting the double is 75% to Black, 25% to White. If the odds are worse than this White is better off refusing. If better than 75/25, White will lose less by accepting.

5 Blocking/Positional Games and Advice on Doubling

Blocking and positional games are the most frequent of all types. Each side battles for position, trying to restrict the other's movement whilst establishing a position of overwhelming advantage.

White wins the opening move and must play 2:1. He elects to try and make his 5 point by playing W6–W5, B12–W11 (*diagram 60*). So long as Black does not hit his blot he has a very high probability of covering on his next turn. Any 3 from W8, any 6 from W11 and any 1 from W6 will cover.

Black throws 5:4. Nothing very constructive can be done with this throw so he immediately decides to hit the blot, moving W1–W5, and brings down one builder W12–B8 with the 5 (*diagram 61*).

This is a reverse for White, though not serious. Black still has an open home board so there will be no difficulty about re-entry, but Black is threatening to gain control of the white 5 point if he throws another 4 on his next turn; or failing that, any 6 will now enable him to hit the white blot on W11.

White throws 3:2, and is faced with a choice very common in backgammon: does he re-enter on B2 and drive Black off his 5 point by playing W8–W5? Or does he re-enter on B3 and cover the blot on W11 by moving the 2 from B12? At the start of the game when White dropped a blot on W5, Black had 15 dice combinations that would enable him to hit the blot from W1. Now if White hits the blot, Black will have 22 chances of hitting the new blot (all the 5s on re-entry, and all the 4s from W1), and two of the chances 6:5 and 5:6 would enable him additionally to hit the white blot on W11. White therefore decides to risk Black

DIAGRAM 60

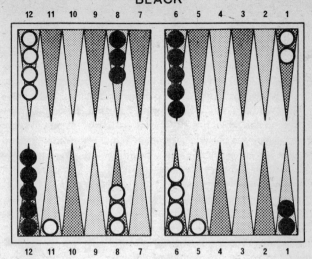

DIAGRAM 61

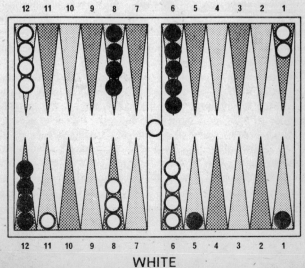

making his 5 point, re-enters on B3, and covers his blot B12–W11 (*diagram 62*).

Black throws 6:3. From his point of view this is a most unsatisfactory throw. He cannot move the man on W5, or cover it. He decides to enhance his blockade-building position by moving W12–B10, leaving his blot 7 points away from the white man on B3. But where does he play the problem 6? If he plays into his own bar point White can hit him from B1 or B3, making it very vulnerable. Equally the alternative of playing into the White bar point is not very attractive. White is now in a position where he has an excellent chance of hitting and covering on W7 or W5. In the end Black decides to play W1–W7, hoping that it will prove to be the lesser of the two evils (*diagram 63*), and that if it is hit it only has to go backwards a few spaces. If he put the blot into his own bar point it would go a long way back, and he would then have three men back instead of only 2.

White studying the board notes that Black has made little progress in building any blockade, but is threatening either to escape with his runners, or to make the white bar point on his next turn. He throws his dice and gets 6:4. He ignores the opportunity to make the black bar point, and uses his move in a policy of trying to trap the black runners by playing B12–W7, W11–W7 to make his own bar point, and places the black blot on the bar (*diagram 64*). So long as Black has a totally open board and virtually no blockade, White does not mind risking the blot on W11. Far more important at this stage is to build up his own blockade.

Black throws 2:1. Another throw he could well have done without! He decides to re-enter on W1 and move onto W3. Any other move would force him to expose yet another blot to White, and he certainly does not want to reduce his blockade-making chances by playing a safe move B10–B8 (*diagram 65*).

White throws 5:2—quite useless for extending his blockade, so the only move worth considering is to hit the black blot on B10, moving B3–B10, thus further reducing Black's blockade-making chances, and sending a third man back to the starting position (*diagram 66*).

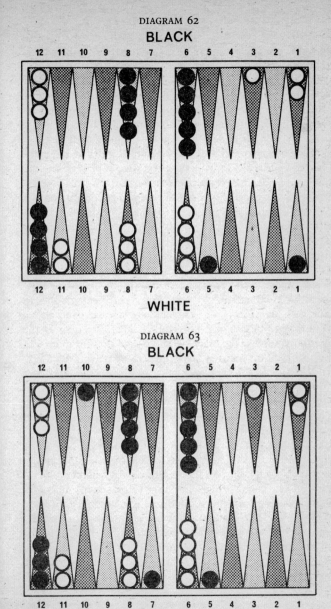

DIAGRAM 62

BLACK

WHITE

DIAGRAM 63

BLACK

WHITE

DIAGRAM 64

BLACK

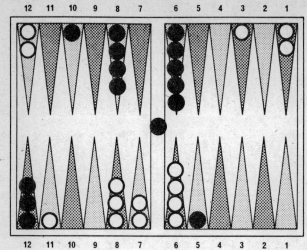

WHITE

DIAGRAM 65

BLACK

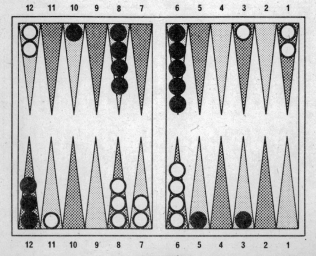

WHITE

DIAGRAM 66

BLACK

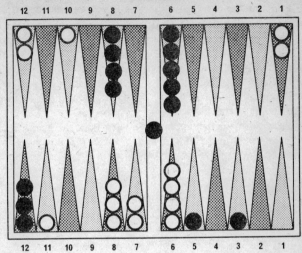

WHITE

DIAGRAM 67

BLACK

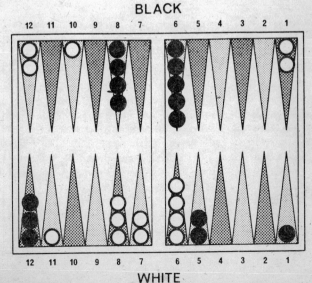

WHITE

Black throws 2:1, re-enters on W1 and moves W3–W5 to secure the white 5 point. Black now quite rightly feels that his runners are secure on a point from which it should not be difficult for them to escape when the time is right. By leaving a man on the W1 point he also makes it dangerous for White to drop a blot behind the 5 point. Though he has made no progress in building his own blockade he does hold a good position in the white home board (*diagram 67*).

White throws 6:3 and plays B1–B10 to make the point. This is taking a risk with the blot on W11, exactly 6 points away from Black on W5. White reasons as follows:

1   If Black attempts to run he has a very high chance of being driven back as long as White holds B12 and B10.
2   If his blot on W11 is hit it may well be the cause of Black losing control of White's vital 5 point. There are no problems of re-entry so this might well end up a satisfactory sacrifice.
3   If Black attempts to drop a blot into his own home board the White man on B1 has an excellent chance of hitting it (*diagram 68*).

Black throws 1:1 and immediately plays two men B8–B7 and two men B6–B5. In one move Black has revolutionised his position, secured control of his 4 most important points and unlike White, started to close up his home board. For the first time in this game Black feels that things are beginning to go his way (*diagram 69*). White now decides that if it is possible he must move or cover his blot on W11, and escape with his runner before Black can extend his blockade any further.

White throws and gets 3:3. So he moves W11–W8 to get the blot safe, B1–B4 to prepare his runner for escape, and two men W6–W3 to start closing his board and to provide a safe landing point for his home-coming men (*diagram 70*).

Black throws 4:2. It would be suicide to run with one of his distant men with White waiting to pounce from B12 and B10. The only logical move is to play B8–B4, B6–B4 to make the

DIAGRAM 68

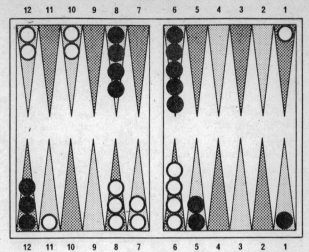

DIAGRAM 69

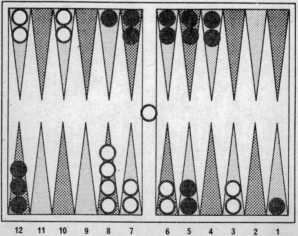

DIAGRAM 70

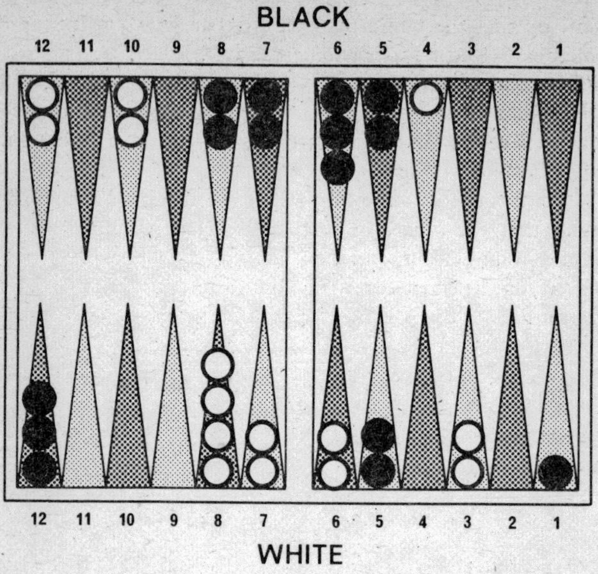

BLACK

WHITE

DIAGRAM 71

BLACK

WHITE

point, putting the white man on the bar, and closing up his home board a little further (*diagram 71*).

White throws 6:4, fails to re-enter his man and forfeits his move. Black throws 5:4. He constructs a 5 point blockade by moving W12–B8, and then starts his runner on the way home moving W1–W5 (*diagram 72*).

White throws 6:5 and again fails to re-enter his man. Black, feeling that the wheel of fortune is really running his way doubles White. White accepts. He reasons that with 3 points open to him he must surely be able to re-enter his man in the near future and Black is not going to find it easy to get his men home past the two points White holds (B12 and B10). Black now throws 6:5. He has two ways to play this. He could risk everything to try and complete a prime, by moving the two men on W12 to B8 and B7, giving him two builders that he hopes will

DIAGRAM 72

BLACK

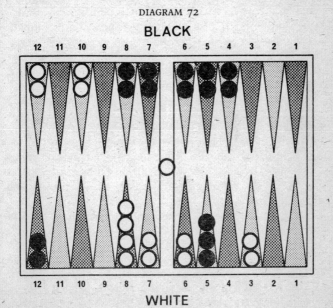

WHITE

complete the prime on the next move. This is, however, a very
risky move. Firstly only 5:4 or 4:5 will enable him to complete
the prime (2 chances out of 36). Secondly if White re-enters and
escapes it is going to be very difficult to hit the white blot once
he gives up the W12 point. Thirdly if he has no safe landing
point on W12 it is going to be very difficult indeed to bring his
last three men home without being hit. Black wisely decides to
play W5–B9. If White gets the lucky 3:6 or 6:3 (2 chances in 36)
he will virtually have lost the game. If White gets one of the
other 34 permutations then Black will be able to complete a
prime with any 4 (11 chances in 36) or with 2:2 or with 6:5 or
5:6 from W5 (*diagram 73*).

White throws 6:2, re-enters his man on B2 and moves
another man W8–W2 (*diagram 74*). So far in the game we have
seen Black, after an adverse start, construct an excellent blockade and he is now close to trapping the white runner behind a
prime. White, having failed to secure a good blocking position,
changed his tactics to play a positional game that makes it difficult for Black to escape with his last two men on W5. Never-
theless White is in a very difficult situation: if he can escape
with his runner he may be in a winning position; but if it is
trapped behind a prime he will certainly lose.

Black throws 6:3. Not exactly the throw he wanted! He decides:

1 Not to move from W12. This point is still vital to help his
   last 2 men escape.
2 Not to move from B9. This blot is 7 points away from the
   white man on B2, and so can only be hit by 6:1 (2 chances
   in 36). Black still hopes to be able to cover the blot and
   complete his prime.
3 He finally decides to run with one man from W5–B11
   (*diagram 75*). If White should get a 1 on his next turn he
   can hit the black man on B11, but cannot, at the same
   time, move his blot B2–B3. White must do this if he is to
   have any hope of escaping with a 6. Therefore, Black
   reasons, White will not dare to hit his blot on B11. In
   addition, by placing his blot on B11, he increases his

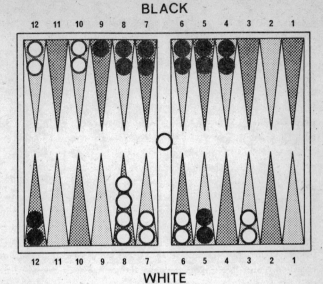

DIAGRAM 73

BLACK

WHITE

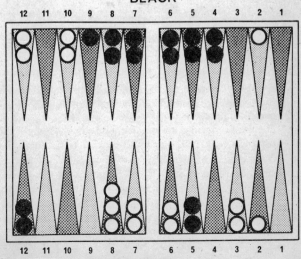

DIAGRAM 74

BLACK

WHITE

DIAGRAM 75

BLACK

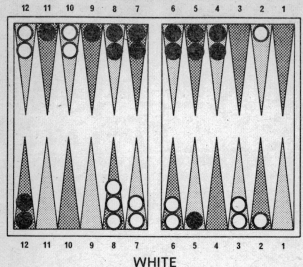

WHITE

chances of covering the blot on B9 with his next turn. Finally if White does make the error of hitting his blot on B11, it is unlikely that he will also be able to cover the blot on W2, giving Black a shot at it during re-entry.

White throws 6:3. He certainly did not want that combination. There is nothing he can do with his trapped runner and White knows that his situation is now desperate. Any combination with a 4 or 2 or 6:5 will enable Black to complete his prime. White's situation is so serious that he must take any risk to try and save the position. He plays W8–W2 to cover his blot with the 6 and W8–W5 to hit the black blot and put it on the bar in a desperate attempt to stop Black making his prime (*diagram 76*).

Black throws 6:2 and cannot re-enter. White's desperate action has given him a brief breathing space. White throws 3:1. He covers his blot on W5 by moving from W8. The problem is the

DIAGRAM 76

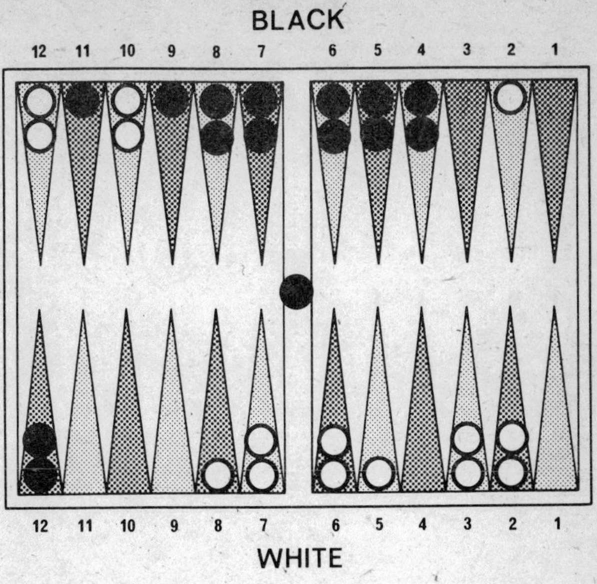

BLACK

WHITE

1. At first he is tempted to hit the blot on B11; with four points closed in his home board Black's chances of re-entering both men fall to a mere 11%. Strong though the temptation is, White resists it and decides he must play B2–B3 so that his trapped man can escape as soon as he throws a 6. In any other circumstances he would have put two black men on the bar (*diagram 77*).

Black throws 4:3. The 4 he so badly wanted to complete his prime must be wasted re-entering his man on W4. What should he now do with the 3? With two blots exposed he must move one of them, but which? There are 11 dice permutations that contain a 6 with which to hit the man on B9. There are also 11 dice permutations that contain a 1 to enable the blot on B11 to be hit. So from the point of view of probability there is nothing to choose between the two blots. Therefore he decides that he must leave a blot in a position, where, if it is not hit, it will most

DIAGRAM 77

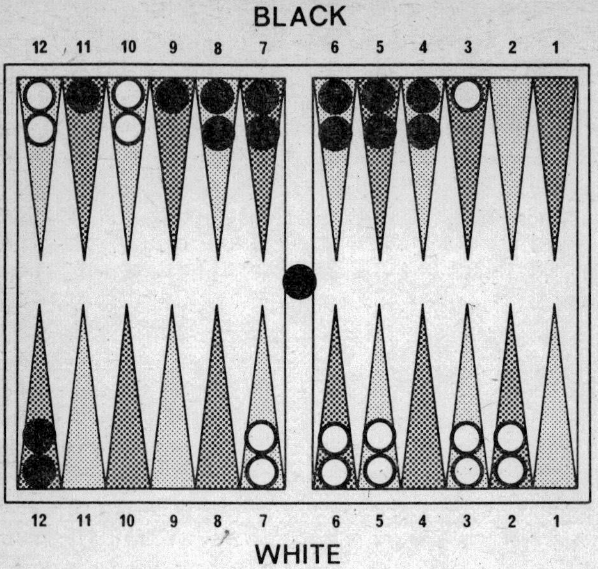

BLACK

12 11 10 9 8 7   6 5 4 3 2 1

WHITE

DIAGRAM 78

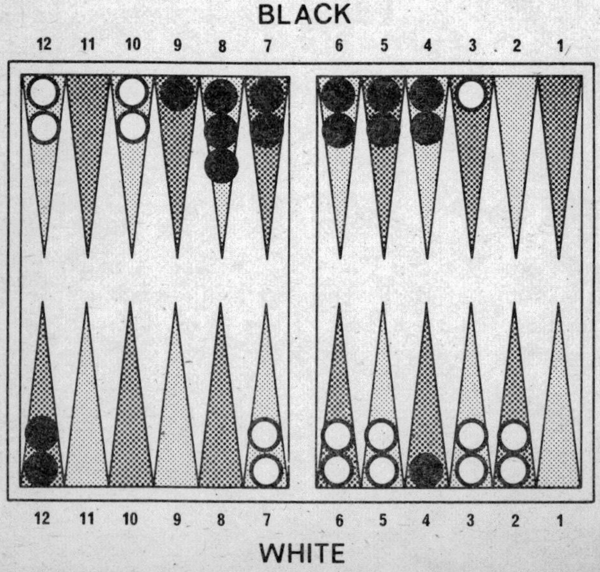

BLACK

12 11 10 9 8 7   6 5 4 3 2 1

WHITE

benefit his position on the next turn. He moves B11–B8, still hoping to make his prime, either by covering the blot on B9, or by playing 6:5, B9–B3, B8–B3 (*diagram 78*).

White throws 6:3. A perfect throw, he hits the black blot and moves onto B12. Note how White does not hit the blot on W4 from W7. Black's 5 point blockade is too dangerous to leave a blot exposed in his home board. A major reverse for Black (*diagram 79*).

Black throws 3:1, enters with the 1 and moves the same man on W1–W4 to make the point. Black's blockade is now of no use unless he can hit a white blot, so now he changes his tactics to playing a positional game, and will not therefore move his men from W12 or W4. Until he can hit White all moves will be played into his home board (*diagram 80*).

White's turn to play. Flushed with the success of the escape of his runner and the dramatic improvement in his position he re-doubles Black, hoping that after such a reverse Black will instantly resign. Instead Black instantly accepts. He in turn reasons that holding the W4 point he is in no real danger of being gammoned, and that the gap between B12 and W7 should with any luck give him a good chance to hit a blot when White brings his men home. White, by now wishing that he had not been so hasty with the re-double throws his dice and gets 5:3, moving B12–W5 (*diagram 81*).

Black throws and gets 5:2, and moves B8–B3, B8–B6. He is intent on closing up his board as fast as possible so that when he does hit a white blot re-entry will be as difficult as possible (*diagram 82*).

White throws 4:1. This is where the gap he has to cross becomes so dangerous; he cannot bring in another man without exposing a blot to Black, so he decides to play safe moving W5–W1, W2–W1 (*diagram 83*).

Black throws 5:4 and moves B8–B3, B6–B2 (*diagram 84*).

White throws 3:1. He does not dare move his distant men, so is again forced to play safe, moving W6–W3, W6–W5 (*diagram 85*). Both sides are playing a cat-and-mouse game, each hoping that the other will be forced to make a run for home first, leav-

DIAGRAM 79
BLACK

WHITE

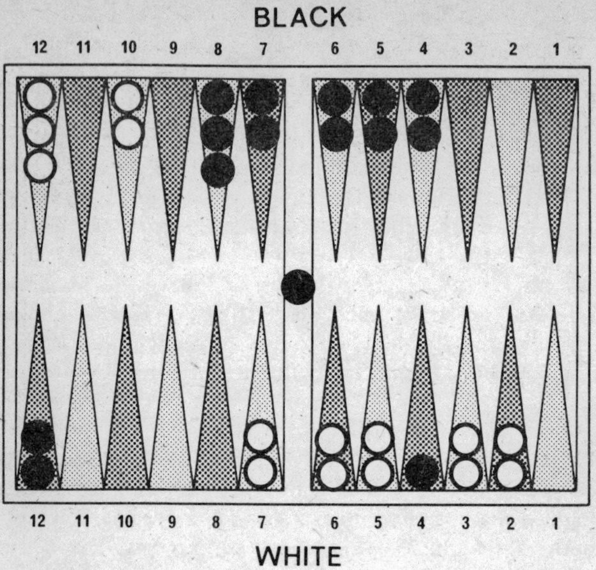

DIAGRAM 80
BLACK

WHITE

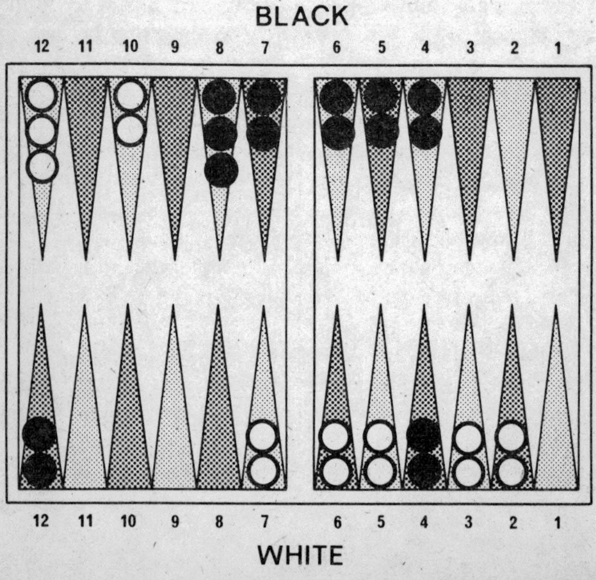

DIAGRAM 81

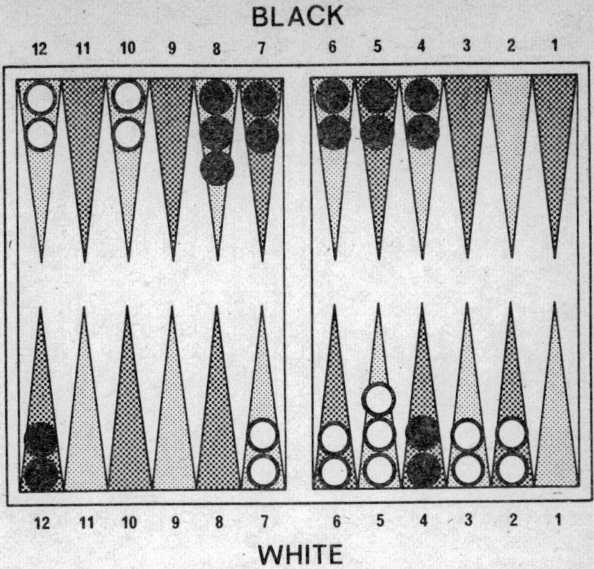

BLACK

WHITE

DIAGRAM 82

BLACK

WHITE

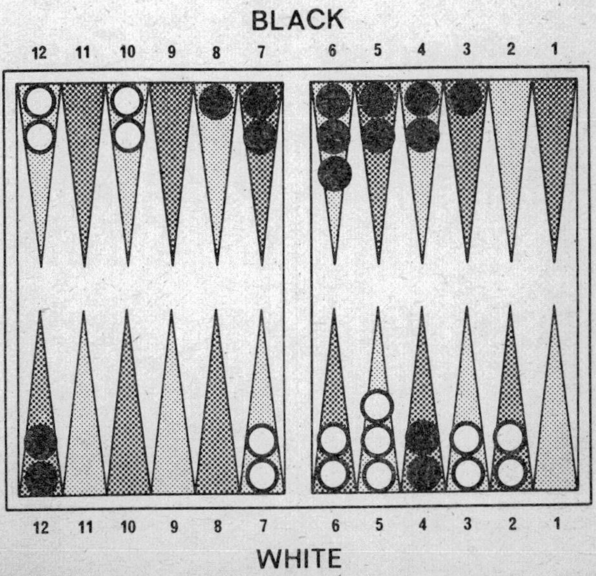

DIAGRAM 83

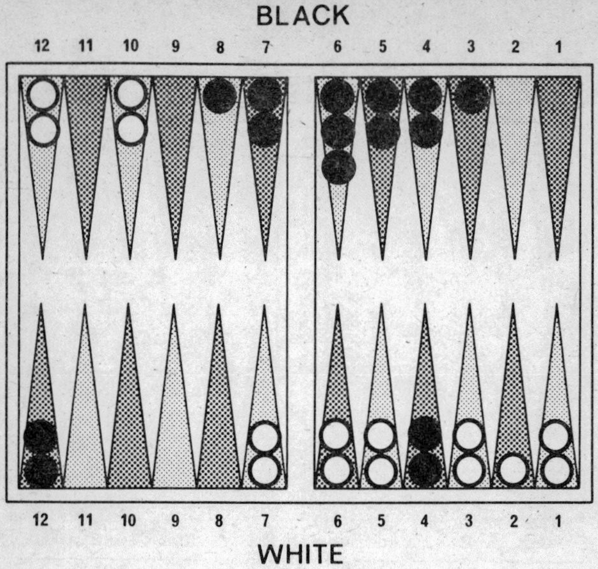

BLACK

12 11 10 9 8 7 6 5 4 3 2 1

12 11 10 9 8 7 6 5 4 3 2 1

WHITE

DIAGRAM 84

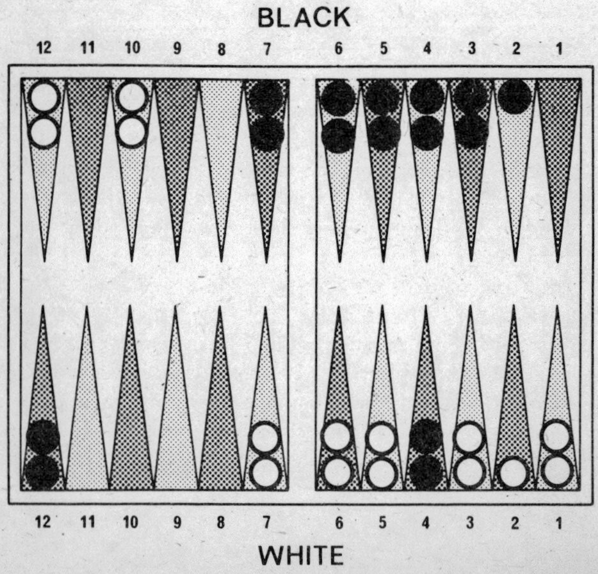

BLACK

12 11 10 9 8 7 6 5 4 3 2 1

12 11 10 9 8 7 6 5 4 3 2 1

WHITE

DIAGRAM 85

BLACK

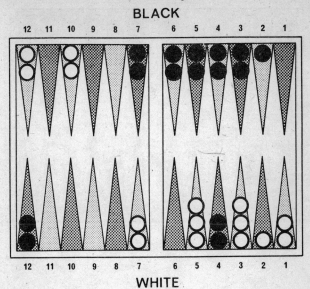

WHITE

ing a blot on the way. The position is moving steadily in Black's favour. White has already been forced to open up a point in his home board, whereas Black is still closing his up.

Black throws 5:2 and plays B7–B2, B3–B1. He does not want to move his remaining man on B7; he is keeping it outside his home board so that if he should throw a 6 he will not have to move one of his distant men, and thereby expose a blot (*diagram 86*).

White again throws 3:1 and plays safe W5–W2, W3–W2 (*diagram 87*).

Black throws 6:2, he moves the 6 B7–B1 and the 2 W4–W6. He selects this move for the 2 because White has no spare builders close at hand with which to hit and point him, and because with these two men split, his chances of hitting a white blot, if one is exposed, are greatly enhanced (*diagram 88*).

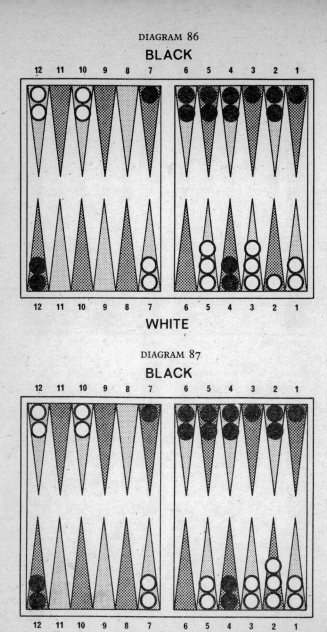

DIAGRAM 86

BLACK

12 11 10 9 8 7   6 5 4 3 2 1

WHITE

DIAGRAM 87

BLACK

12 11 10 9 8 7   6 5 4 3 2 1

WHITE

DIAGRAM 88

BLACK

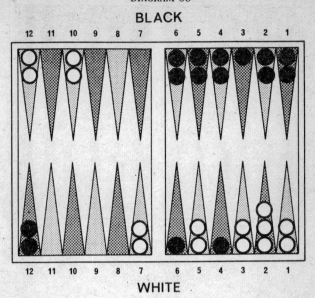

WHITE

White throws a 6:2. The choice is now becoming very difficult. He could play safe by playing from W7 to W1 and W5.
The thing he dislikes about this move is that it increases the gap
that his last four men must cross, and he can be quite sure that
whatever happens Black will keep his men waiting for the white
men to cross that large open space. The alternative would be to
bring home one of his most distant men playing B10–W7, risking being hit whilst Black has a blot exposed in his home board
and no builders waiting to cover it. If Black's home board had
been closed he would have played safe, but with a blot exposed
he decides to risk running (*diagram 89*).

Black throws 6:5, and hits the white blot by moving W4–B10
(*diagram 90*). White throws 5:2 and fails to re-enter. Black now
re-doubles White to 8. This time White refuses. He judges that
Black will either move or cover the blot and that with only one

DIAGRAM 89

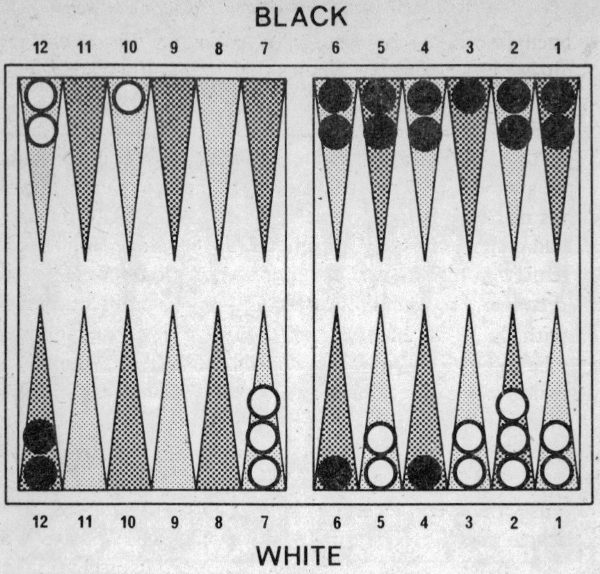

BLACK

| 12 | 11 | 10 | 9 | 8 | 7 | 6 | 5 | 4 | 3 | 2 | 1 |

| 12 | 11 | 10 | 9 | 8 | 7 | 6 | 5 | 4 | 3 | 2 | 1 |

WHITE

DIAGRAM 90

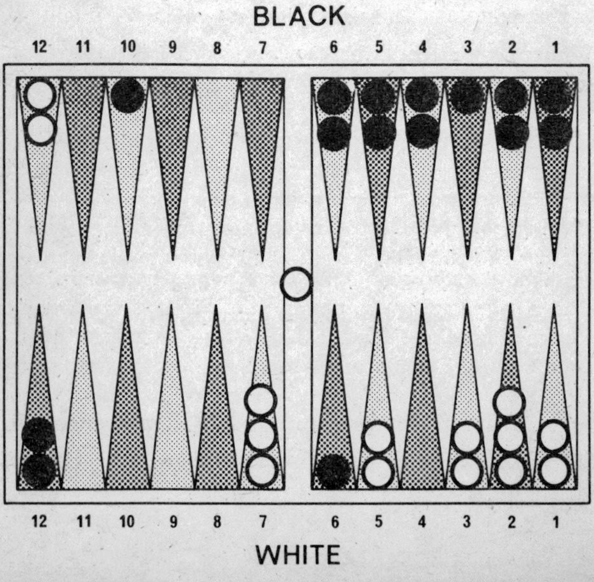

BLACK

| 12 | 11 | 10 | 9 | 8 | 7 | 6 | 5 | 4 | 3 | 2 | 1 |

| 12 | 11 | 10 | 9 | 8 | 7 | 6 | 5 | 4 | 3 | 2 | 1 |

WHITE

point open it will not be easy to re-enter and escape without Black hitting him again. He decides that he would rather pay up 4 than risk losing 8, so the game ends.

This is a good example of a blocking/positional game. Each side struggles to construct a dominant blockade and when that fails, each side switches to a positional game. The major error of the game was made by White, when he re-doubled Black too early. White had control of the doubling cube at that stage, and should not have used it until he was in a more secure position. If he had retained control of the cube Black could not have forced him to resign with the re-double to 8, and though White's position was adverse he might well have hit the blot and won the game.

Possession of the doubling cube is very important, and you should not lightly surrender that right. As long as you hold it no one can force you to resign when the going becomes a little tough; but give up control and you give to your opponent the right to use the psychological advantage of the re-double.

In backgammon there are many situations where experts will totally fail to agree, and probably the offering, accepting or refusal of the double or re-double will cause more disagreement than anything else. In this chapter we showed White offering a double prematurely. Yet against another opponent it might have been the correct thing to do.

The cube is a club, and should be used as such. It is often possible to force an opponent to retire by threatening or bluffing him with a double. You need to study the psychology of your opponent. Some crumble quickly when you double, some hesitate, some almost always accept.

If you are playing an opponent who accepts most doubles, you should not double him until you are certain that the situation is almost watertight. If he is the type who resigns easily then do not hesitate to double him the moment you judge he will resign. The whole object is to win as often as you can, and repeated wins of one point are better than a few wins and several losses of two points. Beware of the opponent who does not crumble easily, and remember that an apparent advantage early in the game can so easily turn out to be nothing more; your lead can evaporate just as quickly as the morning dew in the sun. A good player knows this, and he will be quick to accept the early double; having possession of the cube you can be quite sure that he will be ruthless with the re-double if and when the game moves in his favour.

When you double an opponent, do so with a self-confident and aggressive attitude; it is all part of the bluff to rattle him, to demoralise him. Listen to the comments your opponent makes. If he is complaining about his luck, his bad dice, or saying that he is off form that night, then take them as clues and use the cube more aggressively, and make comments that reinforce his feeling that he is out of luck. If he is in top self-confident form and feeling he is on a winning streak, then be more cautious—he is in a mood where he is more likely to accept.

This psychological use of the cube is very important, but it is also necessary to have some guidelines by which to judge when to double/accept/refuse.

Guidance on doubling

A In the running game, you should double when:

1   You appear to be 2 or 3 turns ahead;
2   Your pip point count is 8% to 10% ahead.

You accept a running game doubled when you are not more than 15% behind.

B In mid-game: mid-game doubles are always for positional reasons, so to double in mid-game you need:

1   A strong block of 4 to 5 consecutive points;
2   2 or 3 of your opponent's men behind your block;
3   Your opponent with a weaker block and/or unlikely to be able to trap your men behind it.

Mid-game doubles require considerable judgement and experience, and there is no easy formula for acceptance or refusal. All positional games can be reversed with luck and skill. Therefore take care not to double too early, your advantage may vanish quickly.

C   In the back game: if your opponent is playing a back game (see next chapter) the chances are that you will be forced to expose a man at some stage of the bearing off process. Therefore you should not double a back game until either his board is breaking up, or until he is forced to weaken his back game by giving up control of one of the two points he holds in your home board. The moment you see his position weakening, double him.

D   In the end game. Double when:

1   The distribution of the men in the home boards is in your favour, *i.e.* if your men are placed on the lower points, whereas his are placed predominantly on the higher points, and particularly if he has a gap in the middle. He will very probably throw the number relating to that gap at some stage, and will have to move instead of taking off one man. Therefore you can value each gap in your opponent's home board as being the equivalent of a lead of one additional man off the board.

2   If positional factors are equal, and you both have the same number of men, the advantage will be with the person whose turn it is to throw the dice. He will be two men ahead after his turn, and (excepting doubles) will almost certainly stay that way. Therefore if you are in this position you double him to force his resignation. There is no point in allowing play to continue, as he might throw a double and catch up with you. If this is done to you, refuse the double.

3   In the last 1 or 2 throws of the dice double if your chances of getting off before your opponent are better than 50%. If this is done to you accept if his chances of winning are not more than 74%.

E   Potential gammon and backgammon situations; where it is likely that you will gammon or backgammon your opponent, do not double. Your double gives him the option to refuse and concede one point to you. Force him to play to the end and win a 2- or 3-point game for the gammon and backgammon respectively.

6 The Back Game

No one ever gets into a back game for choice. They require great skill, judgement and experience to master. A back game almost always results in doubles and if they fail to save you, nearly always end up in a gammon or backgammon.

If you play backgammon regularly it is inevitable that you will from time to time find yourself either defending, or playing a back game, so that it is essential to master the technique thoroughly.

The back game is often caused by a fight developing over a major point, such as the bar point, with repeated hits and counter-hits. When the battle is over, one player is left with several of his men driven into the opponent's home board, and in danger not only of being trapped, but also of being left far behind in a running race; it looks virtually certain that he is in the losing position.

A back game can develop quite suddenly, as we shall see in this next game. Black wins the opening throw with 2:1 and plays W12–B11, B6–B5 in an attempt to gain control of his 5 point (*diagram 91*). White throws 6:4 and hits both blots, moving B1–B11 (*diagram 92*). Black throws 6:4 and enters one man on W4 (*diagram 93*). White throws 4:2 and makes his 4 point putting Black back on the bar with 2 blots (*diagram 94*). Black throws 5:4 and re-enters one man on W5 (*diagram 95*). White throws 1:1 and plays W6–W5 with two men and W8–W7 with two men to complete a 4 point blockade, and with both black men back on the bar (*diagram 96*).

Black's position is looking very bad. Two men on the bar and

DIAGRAM 91

BLACK

12	11	10	9	8	7	6	5	4	3	2	1

WHITE

DIAGRAM 92

BLACK

12	11	10	9	8	7	6	5	4	3	2	1

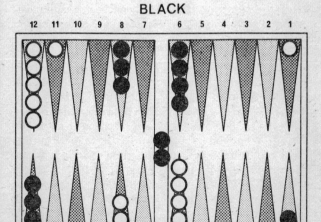

WHITE

DIAGRAM 93

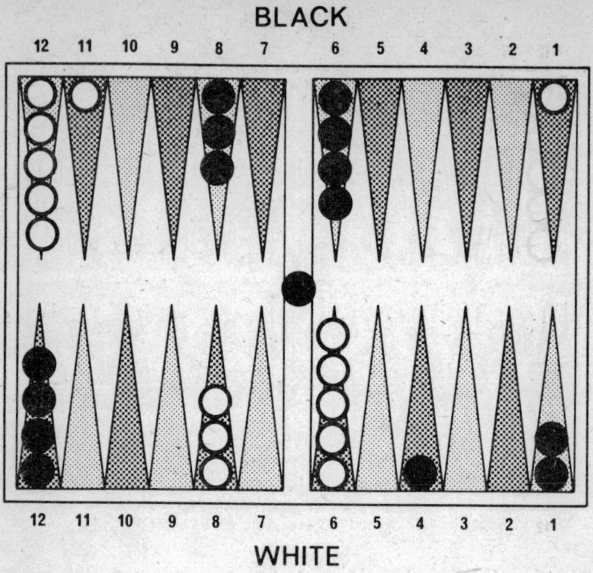

BLACK

WHITE

DIAGRAM 94

BLACK

WHITE

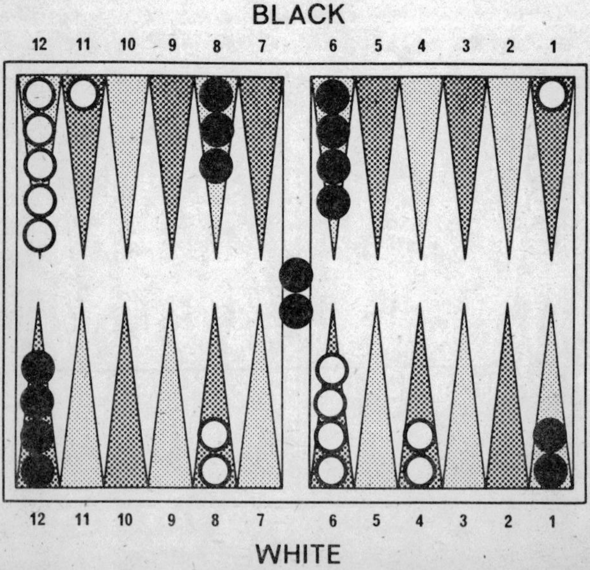

DIAGRAM 95

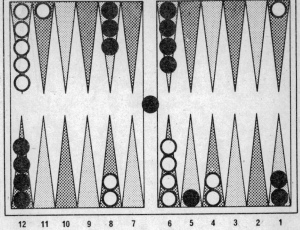

DIAGRAM 96

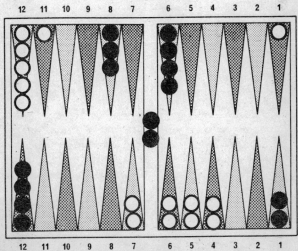

DIAGRAM 97

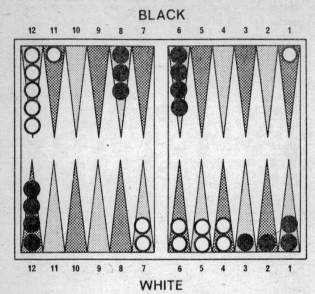

no progress whatsoever. It looks as though White will either double him or play for a gammon. He throws 2:3 and re-enters both men on W2 and W3 (*diagram 97*). White now decides that a four point blockade, a partially closed home board and the total lack of progress on Black's part justify a double. In this instance Black does not instantly accept. He studies the position and notes the following:

1   White has no spare builders nearby so will probably not be able to close up his board any further and/or put Black's men on the bar.

2   If he had still one or two men on the bar he would probably refuse the double, but now it should be possible to escape with two of his men, who with luck might well make a point the other side of the white blockade and be a

constant thorn in his side when he brings his men home. If that fails it should be possible to turn his position into a back game situation.

3 If he is forced into a back game, the advance of his own men into his home board is very delayed, so that again, with a bit of luck to help, by the time he hits a white blot his home board will be tightly closed up.

4 He rates possession of the cube as a major advantage and judges that being able to pressurise White by re-doubling to 4 at the right moment is worth the risks involved.

He therefore accepts the double. White throws his dice and gets 6:5, playing B11–W8, B12–W8 to construct a 5-point blockade (*diagram 98*). Black now gives up all hope of escape,

DIAGRAM 98

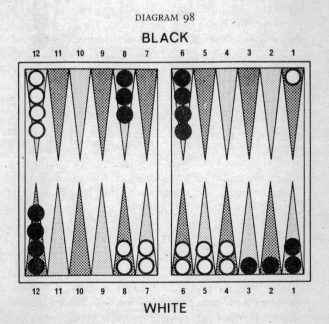

and decides that like it or not he must play a back game. To play
a successful back game you need:

1   To hold two points in your opponent's home board.
2   To have not less than five men on those two points.
3   To have the development of your own home board very
    retarded.

Black throws his dice and gets 6:1. No longer does he use this
throw to make his own bar point, instead he first plays W2–W3
to gain control of a second point in White's home board. This
fulfils the first requirement of a back game. Now he must
somehow get at least one more man back so that he has not less
than five men on those two points. So he plays W12–B7 in the
hope that the blot will be hit by the white runner (*diagram 99*).

White, realising that Black is playing a back game, does not
intend to do anything to help Black improve his position. He
will do his utmost not to hit another black blot, and will also try
to tempt Black to destroy his back game position. He throws his
dice and gets 6:1 and plays B12–W6 (*diagram 100*).

Black throws 3:2 and immediately exposes 2 more blots in a
determined attempt to make White hit him, by playing B8–B5,
B6–B4 (*diagram 101*). White throws 3:1. He cannot move his runner without hitting a black blot, so he decides to try and tempt
Black out of his back game position by playing B12–W9, leaving
a blot exactly 6 spaces away from the black men on W3 (*diagram
102*). White hopes with this move to achieve the following:

1   If he can tempt Black to hit him, it will break up his back
    game position, and there will be no difficulty about re-
    entry. Black's home board is wide open.
2   He then anticipates pointing Black rapidly on W3, and
    hitting a lot of black blots in Black's home board, so that
    he will have so many men off the board that it will be very
    difficult to re-enter them. If this comes off he is certain of
    a gammon, and a backgammon would be within reach.

Black throws and gets 6:5. He refuses the temptation of hitting White on W9. There is no point in hitting the blot at this

DIAGRAM 99

BLACK

| 12 | 11 | 10 | 9 | 8 | 7 | 6 | 5 | 4 | 3 | 2 | 1 |

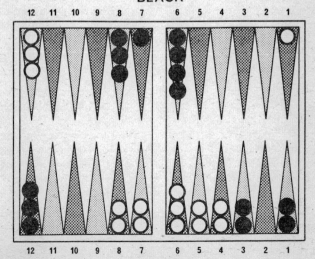

| 12 | 11 | 10 | 9 | 8 | 7 | 6 | 5 | 4 | 3 | 2 | 1 |

WHITE

DIAGRAM 100

BLACK

| 12 | 11 | 10 | 9 | 8 | 7 | 6 | 5 | 4 | 3 | 2 | 1 |

| 12 | 11 | 10 | 9 | 8 | 7 | 6 | 5 | 4 | 3 | 2 | 1 |

WHITE

DIAGRAM 101

BLACK

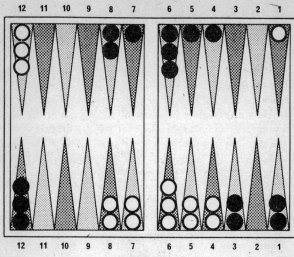

WHITE

DIAGRAM 102

BLACK

WHITE

stage; it could not be trapped in his home board. The only throw that might have tempted him would be a 6:6. Therefore he continues with his aim of forcing White to hit another blot by playing B8–B2 and B6–B1, to place White on the bar (*diagram 103*). White throws 4:1 and has no option; he must hit a black blot. He re-enters on B4 and plays W9–W8 with the 1 (*diagram 104*).

Black throws 6:4 and cannot re-enter. This does not worry him. He still has plenty of time on his side, and the loss of a throw ensures that he does not develop his home board too early in the game. White throws 6:4 and makes W2 by moving W8–W2, W6–W2. He will need control of this point as an extra landing point for his returning men (*diagram 105*).

Black throws 3:2. He re-enters his man on W3 to complete a perfect back game position, and then starts on the final requirement, building up a closed home board by moving B7–B5 to make his 5 point (*diagram 106*).

White throws 6:4 and plays B4–W11 (*diagram 107*).

Black throws 5:1 and plays W12–B8, B2–B1 (*diagram 108*).

White throws 6:5 and plays B12–W7, B12–W8 (*diagram 109*).

Black throws 6–4 and brings down 2 more builders playing W12–B7, W12–B9 (*diagram 110*).

White throws 6:1 and plays W11–W5, W7–W6 (*diagram 111*).

Black throws 6:3 and drops one blot into his home board, B9–B3 and brings in a builder by moving B8–B5 (*diagram 112*).

White throws 4:4 and moves 3 men W8–W4 and one man W6–W2 (*diagram 113*).

Black throws 5:6. He covers his blot with the 5, B8–B3, and now uses the spare man on W3 to absorb the 6, moving W3–W9 (*diagram 114*).

White throws 2:1 and brings his last two men into his home board W7–W5, W7–W6 (*diagram 115*).

Black throws 3:1 and makes his 4 point, B7–B4, B5–B4. With his board almost closed up he is now ready to hit a white blot (*diagram 116*).

White throws 4:4, moves one man W6–W2 and removes three men from W4 (*diagram 117*).

Black throws 5:4 and moves W9–B7 (*diagram 118*).

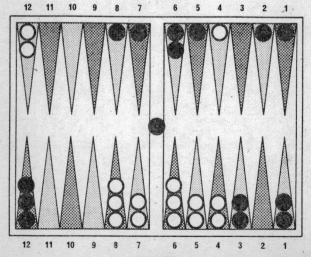

DIAGRAM 103

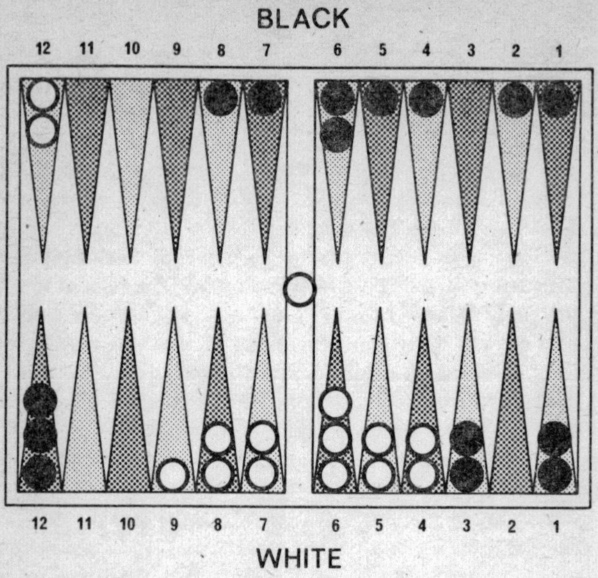

BLACK
12 11 10 9 8 7 6 5 4 3 2 1
12 11 10 9 8 7 6 5 4 3 2 1
WHITE

DIAGRAM 104

BLACK
12 11 10 9 8 7 6 5 4 3 2 1
12 11 10 9 8 7 6 5 4 3 2 1
WHITE

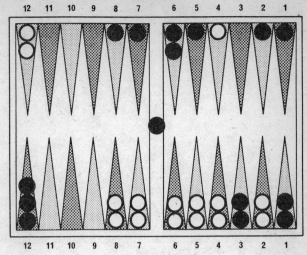

DIAGRAM 105

BLACK

WHITE

DIAGRAM 106

BLACK

WHITE

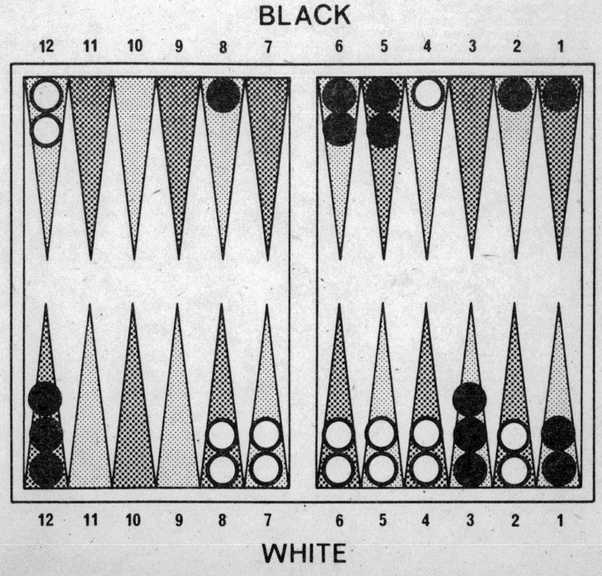

DIAGRAM 107

BLACK

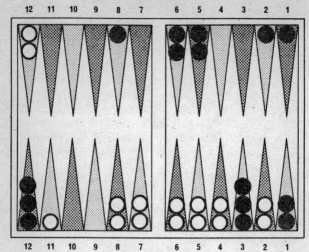

WHITE

DIAGRAM 108

BLACK

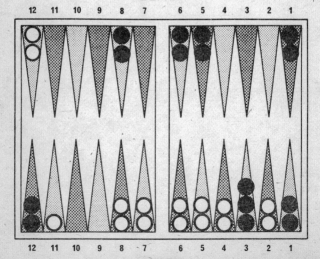

WHITE

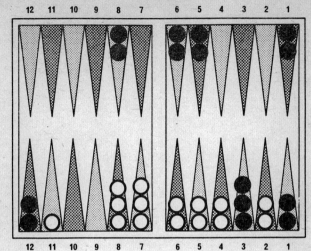

DIAGRAM 109

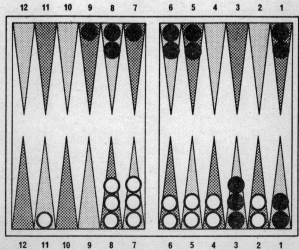

DIAGRAM 110

DIAGRAM 111

BLACK

WHITE

DIAGRAM 112

BLACK

WHITE

DIAGRAM 113

BLACK

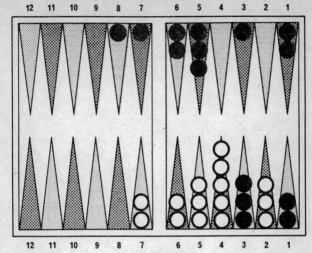

WHITE

DIAGRAM 114

BLACK

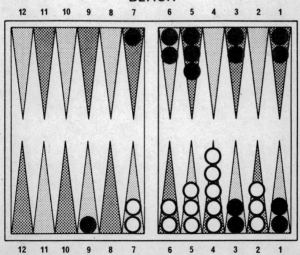

WHITE

DIAGRAM 115

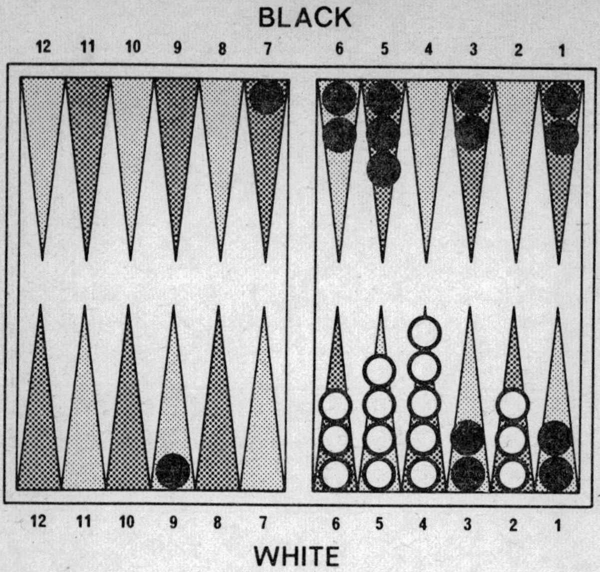

DIAGRAM 116

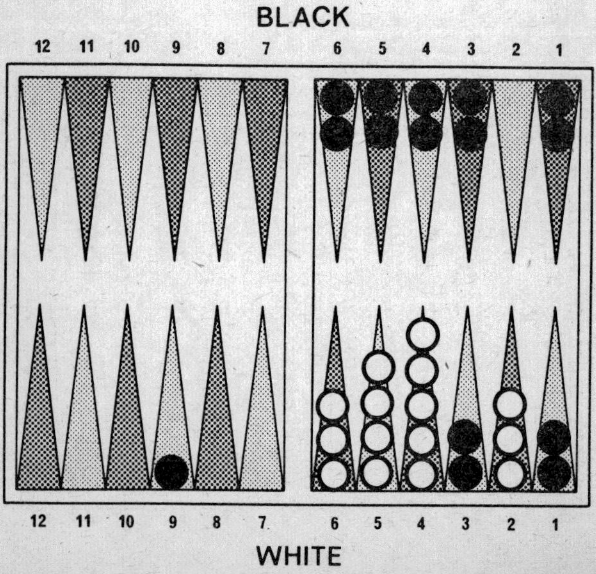

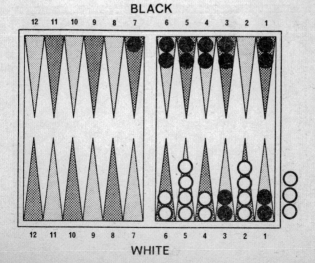

DIAGRAM 117

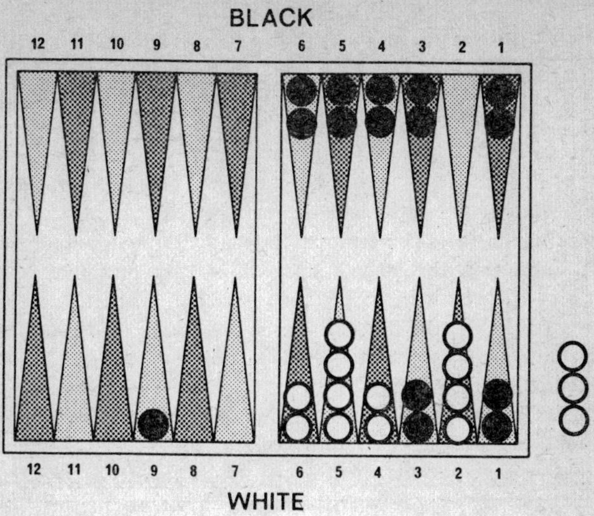

BLACK
12
11
10
9
8
7
6
5
4
3
2
1
12
11
10
9
8
7
6
5
4
3
2
1
WHITE

DIAGRAM 118

BLACK
12
11
10
9
8
7
6
5
4
3
2
1
12
11
10
9
8
7
6
5
4
3
2
1
WHITE

White throws 6:3. He is forced to remove one man from W6 and cannot move the 3 with the remaining man on W6 so is forced to leave a blot. He moves W5–W2 with the 3 (*diagram 119*).

At last Black's opportunity has arrived: any dice combinations containing a 5 or a 3 must hit the blot. The odds are in his favour, but he does not make the mistake of re-doubling White. There are still 16 dice permutations that will miss the blot, so if he re-doubles at this stage White will accept, and failure to hit the blot will result in an instant re-double. Black throws and gets 5:5. He hits the blot and rushes the same man round the board to be ready to assist with closing up the last open point in his board (*diagram 120*).

White throws and fails to re-enter his man. Black promptly re-doubles White to 4. White declines the re-double. Firstly he has to re-enter his man, secondly he has to escape from Black's rapidly closing board, and even having done this Black has three further men that will be lying in wait to drive him back.

This has been an example of a perfect back game, well-timed and with both sides playing with skill, refraining from hitting blots at the wrong time. Because back games invariably involve doubles and re-doubles it is necessary to examine some likely situations that have not come up in this sample game. Look at *diagram 121*. White has just been forced to expose a blot. If it is hit Black will probably double. Should White accept? You must assume that Black will close his board, and that White will not be able to re-enter until Black opens up a point as he bears off his men. With nine men off what are White's chances of winning? Work it out this way:

1 Black will probably get one or two men off before he is forced to open a point.
2 When he does open a point White's chances of re-entry are 11 in 36, so you must assume that White will not re-enter until his second attempt. By this time Black will have four or five men off.

DIAGRAM 119

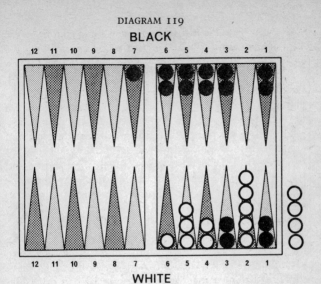

DIAGRAM 120

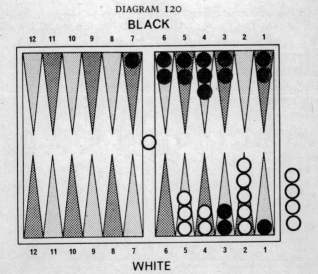

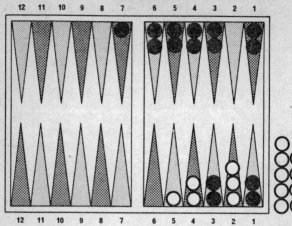

DIAGRAM 121

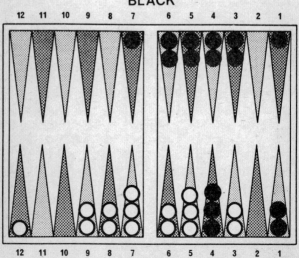

DIAGRAM 122

3   It is going to take White $1\frac{1}{2}$ to 2 turns to get his man back
    to his home board, by which time Black will have between
    seven and eight men off.

Therefore your guideline in this situation is that you refuse
the double unless you have more than half your men off the
board. In this instance you would accept. If you have two men
on the bar you always refuse. To re-enter and bring two men
round the board makes your position hopeless even if you only
have two men left in your home board.

Equally with the situation in *diagram 121* White does not
double if Black fails to hit. With luck White will win by at least
a gammon, if not a backgammon. If Black hits one of the last
white men, White can then promptly double Black and he will
refuse.

Now look at *diagram 122*. Once again Black has the first two
requirements of a back game, having five men back and holding
two points in White's home board. But in this case White
should double him. Black's home board is far too advanced, and
by the time he hits one of White's blots he is going to be forced
to move down in his board, probably leaving the 6 and 5 points
vacant. Re-entry will prove no problem when a blot is hit. In
such a position Black should refuse the double.

Back games are difficult to win, and no one goes into one if he
has any alternative. Judgement of the position cannot be fully
explained by reading a book and to become expert at the back
game requires a great deal of experience.

7 End Play

A great many mistakes can be made in end play, so you need to familiarise yourself with the correct principles of play in five different situations:

1 Closed board, opponent on the bar;
2 Opponent holds your one point;
3 You hold opponent's one point;
4 Opponent playing a back game;
5 The bearing off race.

Closed board, opponent on the bar

Look for a moment at *diagram 123*. What a happy moment for White! The first thing White does in this situation, if the cube is in his possession, is to double Black. Black has only one man on the bar and the rest of his men safely in his home board, so there is no hope of a gammon. So why risk making an error? Double Black first, and unless he is a hopeless gambler he will refuse. Let us suppose that Black holds the cube and you must continue to play. You throw the dice and get 5:4. At first sight, 5:4 appears a safe throw and it does not seem to matter much how you move it. Yet the wrong move now can be a fatal error. The problem is how to move it so that on the following throw you can play a high double, such as 6:6 or 5:5 without exposing a blot to Black. Before reading any further, set out this situation on your own board, and work out the correct move, so that after you have completed it you can play 6:6 or 5:5 in safety.

A move B12–W4 is a correct move, but there are many incorrect ones, such as B12–W8, W10–W6. After such a move 6:6

DIAGRAM 123

BLACK

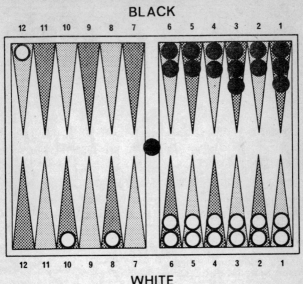

WHITE

will expose a blot. W10–W1 would also be wrong; you could not now play 6:6 or 5:5 without exposing a blot.

Once all your men are in the home board, the easiest way to check your end play is to memorise the safe and dangerous patterns of men on the board. *Diagram 124* illustrates a safe pattern. 6:6, 5:5 or 6:5 can all be played in complete safety. *Diagram 125* illustrates another safe pattern, again 6:6, 5:5 or 6:5 can be played in complete safety. Note that in both the last two diagrams, the number of men on the 6 and 5 point add up to an even number. If you get uneven numbers of men on the 6 and 5 points you could be in trouble. *Diagrams 126 and 127* illustrate two such dangerous patterns of men.

Try to play 6:6 or 5:5 in either diagram, or in the case of diagram 126 even a 6:5. In every case you will be forced to expose a blot. In contrast, *diagram 128* illustrates a safe pattern

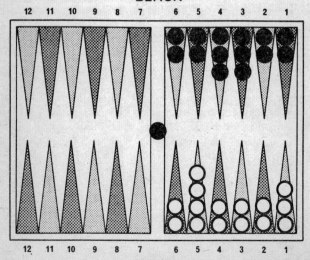

DIAGRAM 124

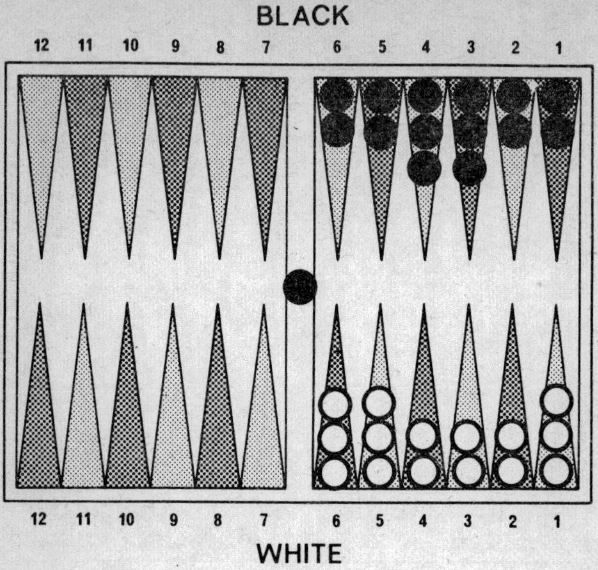

BLACK

12 11 10 9 8 7   6 5 4 3 2 1

12 11 10 9 8 7   6 5 4 3 2 1

WHITE

DIAGRAM 125

BLACK

12 11 10 9 8 7   6 5 4 3 2 1

12 11 10 9 8 7   6 5 4 3 2 1

WHITE

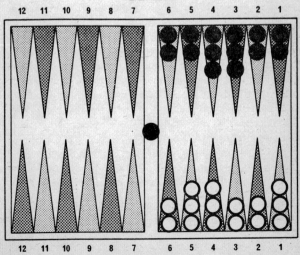

DIAGRAM 126

DIAGRAM 127

DIAGRAM 128
BLACK

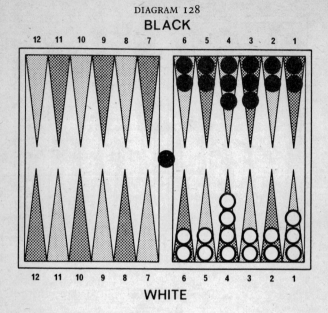

WHITE

in which you can play any dice combination in complete safety. Note once again that the total number of men on the 6 and 5 points add up to an even number.

With an opponent waiting on the bar, the correct play is first of all to move your three surplus men down to the lower points, and then, when you commence to break your home board, always do this from the highest point, taking off and moving down, so that no gap ever appears between the men.

In *diagram 128* you would play 6:4 by removing the 6 and moving the other man W6–W2.

There is one exception to this rule, and it is the only time that you do not break your board from the highest point. In *diagram 129* you throw 5:1. There are two choices open to you:

1 Move W6–W1, W6–W5 or
2 Remove one man from W5, and move the other man

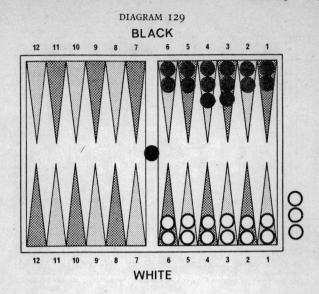

DIAGRAM 129

BLACK

WHITE

W5–W4. 5:1 in this situation is an unlucky throw that puts you at risk.

Both possible solutions are unsatisfactory, but (1) is far worse than (2). In the case of (1) you will expose a blot on your following turn if you throw 6:6, 6:5, 6:4, 6:3, 6:2, 6:1, 5:6, 5:5, 5:4, 5:3, 5:2, 5:1, 4:6, 4:5, 4:4, 3:6, 3:5, 2:6, 2:5, 1:6, 1:5—a total of 21 adverse permutations of the dice.

In the case of (2) you will expose a blot on your next turn if you throw 6:6, 6:1, 5:5, 5:1, 4:4, 4:1, 1:6, 1:5, 1:4—a total of 9 adverse dice permutations.

Diagram 130 illustrates another dangerous pattern. If you have any choice, try to avoid ending up with 3 men on your highest point. 6:5, 6:4, 5:6, 5:4, *etc.* would all force you to expose a blot, and even with five men off the board, if you are hit, you are almost certain to lose the game.

Diagram 131 illustrates a mistake that is very frequently made

DIAGRAM 130

BLACK

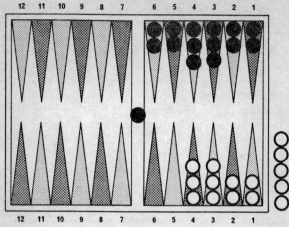

WHITE

DIAGRAM 131

BLACK

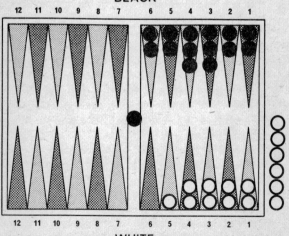

WHITE

by inexperienced backgammon players. You have probably
ended up in this situation by incorrect play a move or two back,
and you were forced to expose a blot, which, much to your
relief, was not hit when Black threw 3:4 and was unable to re-
enter his man. Now you throw 5:1 and with delight remove the
man on W5; but how do you now play the 1 without again
exposing a blot? There is no safe way to play it, a blot must be
exposed. Now put back the man you took off W5 and start
again. First of all remember that there is no rule in backgammon
that states that the higher die must be played before the lower
die. So this time play the 1 first by moving W5–W4 and then
you play the 5 to remove the same man from the board. In this
way no blot is exposed. It's simple when you know it, but so
easy to forget in the heat and excitement of the moment.

Opponent holds your one point

In many ways this situation is the opposite of having an opponent on the bar. Your opponent is so far behind in the game that
he will stay on your one point as long as possible in the hope
that he can reverse the situation by hitting one blot. To expose
one blot to your opponent is bad enough, but if you expose two
to him disaster is virtually certain. *Diagram 132* illustrates the
most dreaded situation. Throw a 6:5 and two blots must be
exposed. Memorise this position and try never to get yourself
into it.

So, unlike the opponent on the bar situations, where correct
play is to get your surplus men down to the lowest points before
you begin to bear off, here you try to place your surplus men on
to your highest points.

In *diagram 133* you have all your men piled onto your top
points. Now you can play high throws by removing men from
the high points, and low throws by moving down from the
higher points to the lower ones. All the time you play safe
moves, hoping that your opponent will soon be forced to remove
one of his troublesome men by throwing a 6 that cannot be
moved anywhere else on the board. If the opportunity arises do

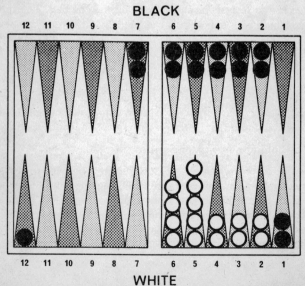

DIAGRAM 134

BLACK

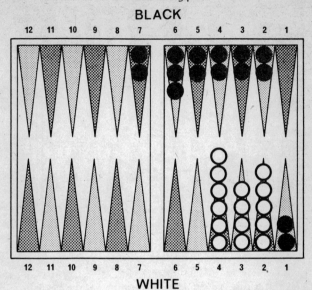

not be in a hurry to remove your men from the board, but pile them up on the lower points into a safe position as illustrated in *diagram 134*. Now the possibility of your exposing a blot before Black is forced to move out is very remote. You will have ample time to remove your men and win once Black starts on the journey home, so in the meantime play with safety.

You hold opponent's one point

Diagram 135 illustrates a situation where greed and prudence fought a battle in your opponent's mind, and greed has won. He decides to go all out to gammon you, so having thrown 4:4 he decides to remove 4 men from his 4 point. The danger that lies in front of him is the gap in his ranks on the four point, and that gap may well force him to expose a blot.

DIAGRAM 135

BLACK

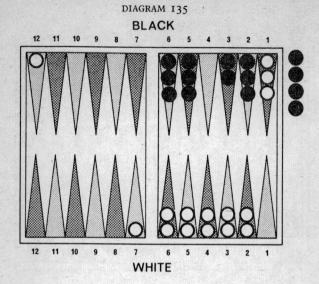

WHITE

You throw 6:3. You must play into the gap he has left, and naturally you move the 6 by playing B12–W7, to complete a prime. By placing a man on B4 you greatly enhance your chances of hitting a black blot, should he expose one. If Black now throws 6:4 he must leave a blot on B6, and your choice of move has greatly increased your chances of hitting, and winning the game.

Diagram 136 illustrates another situation, almost certainly brought about by a greedy attempt to win either a gammon or a backgammon. The more gaps your opponent opened up between you and his men, the greater the likelihood that he will be forced to expose a blot. In this situation you throw a 6:1. The correct play is not to panic and run with one man to try and save yourself from a backgammon. You play the 6 into your home-board, and with the 1 you split your two back men so that they occupy the 1 and 2 points. On his next turn only 6:6, 5:5, 4:4, 3:3, 4:1, 1:4, 3:2, 2:3 can save him from exposing a blot. All

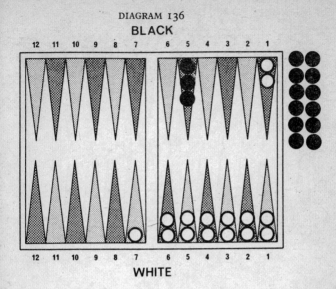

DIAGRAM 136
BLACK

WHITE

other throws will force him to expose between one and three blots. The throw you would like best would, of course, be 2:4. Then he must expose three blots. Your back men are split and must almost certainly hit one or more. If you only hit one you will not save the game, but you will save a gammon. If you can hit two you will very likely win the game.

In *diagram 137* White's situation is not so good. This is an example of an opponent who has played with caution, and you are now in real danger of being backgammoned. There is only one point in your favour: he has an odd number, three men left on the two point. The chances are that, with the exception of a double, he will almost certainly leave one blot on his next turn. So in this situation you run with one man so that if you fail to hit his blot on your next turn you have some hope of being able to get your last man out of his home board to save the backgammon. There is also another reason for moving one man out. So long as you have two men on the one point your opponent does

DIAGRAM 137

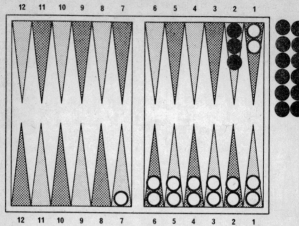

DIAGRAM 138

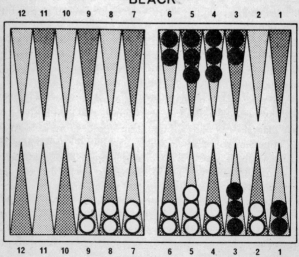

not have to play a 1. By moving out you now force him to play the 1 by taking you off. For example if he throws 4:1, and you have not moved one man out, he removes the 4 and does not have to play the 1. If you have moved one man out and he gets 4:1, he removes one man with the 4 and now must take you off with the 1, exposing two blots to you when you re-enter.

Opponent playing a back game

In *diagram 138* your opponent is in an ideal back game situation holding your 1 and 3 points with a surplus man on the 3 point, which he hopes will escape and move slowly round the board whilst he waits for you to expose a blot. If you now throw 5:3 how do you move it? You have two safe choices:

1   Move 5:3 with the two men on W9 or
2   Move with the two men on W7.

Your instinct will probably tell you to move the two most distant men so that you do not open up a gap in your ranks, which as we have already discovered increases the chances that you may be forced to expose a blot. In a back game situation the same reasons do not apply. You have to be lucky not to expose a blot in a back game, and there is nothing you can do about this luck. The main consideration is not the probability of exposing a blot; instead you should ask yourself how you can force your opponent to destroy his back game position as early as possible, hopefully before you are forced to expose a blot to him. As you study diagram 138 you will note that if you do move from W9 your opponent will now be able to play any 6 by escaping with his one surplus man on W3, whilst leaving his back game situation intact. If, however, you play the 5:3 from W7 he will be forced to play his sixes by moving a man from W1. This is exactly what you want. The moment he does this his back game position is destroyed, and you should quickly be able to hit his blot and cover your man on the 1 point.

In a back game situation, select the moves that enhance the

chances of your opponent being forced to destroy his own position, rather than playing for maximum safety.

The bearing off race

There is nothing very difficult about this stage of the game. It is mainly mechanical, so long as you adhere to a few simple rules:

1   Remove a man from the board, rather than move within the board.
2   When you have to move a man, select the move that fills in a vacant point. In *diagram 139* we show Black and White each with five men on their 6 and 5 points. Let us make both of them play the same throws. In *diagram 140* 4:4 is played correctly by Black; he has filled in two vacant points. White has mistakenly moved four men off his 6 point with the idea that it will help him to win if he empties his top points before Black. Now any throw containing a 1 will enable Black to get a man off the board, whereas White will have to move within his board and will fall one man behind in the race.

In *diagram 141* the throw is 2:1. Again we show Black moving correctly to fill in two vacant points, and White has moved incorrectly.

There is only one situation in which you do not follow the two basic rules for the bearing off race. In *diagram 142* you, as White, are behind in the race. You have just thrown 6:1; how should you play it? Normally you would remove one man from W5 with the 6, and move W2–W1 with the 1, to fill in a vacant point.

This situation is an exception. You can see that whatever happens your opponent will be off the board in 3 turns, which means that after this turn you will have only 2 throws with which to get all your men off the board. You are a certain loser, unless you get a lucky double. Therefore you select the move to increase the chances of removing four men in one go, should you be fortunate enough to get a double.

DIAGRAM 139

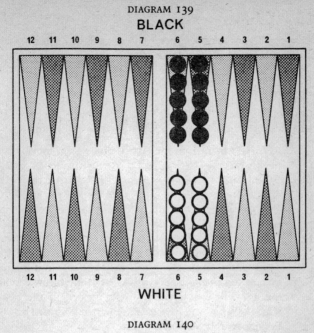

DIAGRAM 140

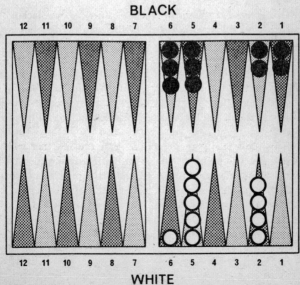

DIAGRAM 141

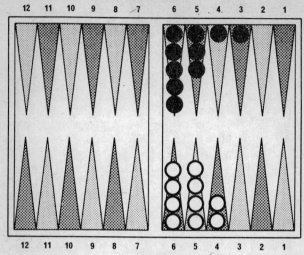

DIAGRAM 142

DIAGRAM 143

BLACK

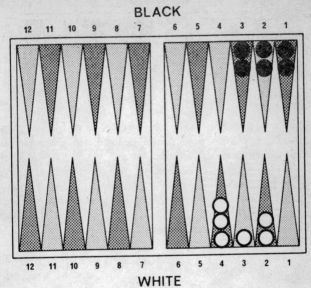

WHITE

With the 6:1 you now remove one man from W5, and move W5–W4 (*diagram 143*). By doing this you can now get 4 men off the board with 6:6, 5:5, 4:4. Had you played the normal way only 6:6, 5:5 will get four men off the board. By selecting this move you have increased your chances of winning by about 3%—not a great deal by itself, but if in your play, game after game, you are always selecting positions that marginally increase your chances of winning, you can be quite sure that the laws of probability will work in your favour, and you will become one of those players who win more often than they lose.

8 Duplication and Non-Duplication

It is of course impossible to win every game of backgammon, but it is quite possible to win more than you lose, so that overall you become a consistent winner.

Duplication and non-duplication are very important aids to winning. The moves selected on these principles are so inconspicuous that many backgammon players, even after years of playing, remain unaware of them. They put their opponent's wins down to luck and never grasp the secrets behind the selected moves.

Duplication

A simple example of duplication may be seen in *diagram 144*. Here White has thrown a 4:1; how should he play it? The correct play is to move B12–W8 (*diagram 145*). Should Black get a 4 he will have to use it to re-enter his man and will not be able to hit the White blot which is exactly 4 spaces away. (Of course, if Black gets the miracle 4:4, White can correctly conclude that luck is on the side of his opponent!) If White had left his blot on W9, Black would have been able to re-enter with a 4 and hit the blot with either 5:4 or 4:5—2 chances in 36. By placing the man on W8, Black can now only enter and hit with 4:4—1 chance in 36. By making use of duplication White reduces Black's slim chances of entering and hitting the blot by a further 50%.

Exactly the same principle applies if you are forced to expose two blots. The dangers of having two blots hit at the same time and the difficulties of re-entry are so great that it is essential to do anything to reduce the risk to the absolute minimum.

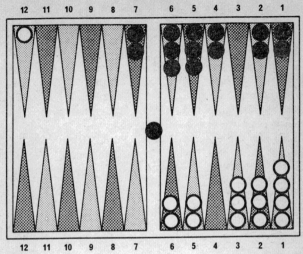

DIAGRAM 144

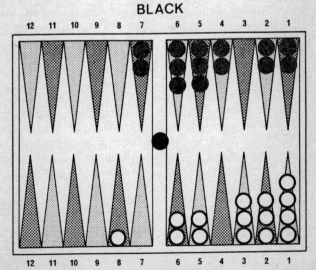

DIAGRAM 145

Duplication can often be used to solve this problem. *Diagram 146* is an example of duplication in a two blot situation. White has just thrown 5:3. There is nothing that White can do to cover his blot on W3, so he plays the 5 by moving B5–B10 and the 3 W7–W4 as in *diagram 147*. Now Black can only hit both blots with the 1 in 36 throw of 3:3. Had he left the blot where it is, or moved it to B8, there are quite a large number of throws that enable Black to hit both blots. Duplication has again reduced the chances of two blots being hit to 1 in 36.

In *diagram 148* White throws 6:1 and decides to make use of duplication at a period when he needs to expose three blots. First he hits the Black blot on B10 with the 6 and then he moves the blot on W4, which he cannot cover, to W3, as in *diagram 149*. Once again Black must use any 3 to re-enter his man and will not be able to hit the blots on B4 or B10. The miracle 3:3 will of course cost you the game, but this one throw excepted, Black has no hope of hitting two blots at the same time on his next turn.

In *diagram 150* White again throws 6:1. He uses his 6 to extricate his last man from the Black home board, but how should he play the 1? Again he must make use of duplication. In *diagram 151* you see how White carefully leaves his man on B7 where it can only be hit by a 6 and plays the 1 W4–W3. If Black uses his 6 to hit the blot it will be at the expense of extricating his last man from the White home board. In the circumstances he cannot risk leaving his man in your trap; he must take it out with any 6 and will not (except with 6:6) be able to hit the blot. If White had moved his blot to B8 with the 1, Black would have been able to hit it with any 5, as well as removing his man with any 6.

Form the habit of looking for situations where duplication can be turned to your advantage. If you have an opponent on the bar always pause before you select your move to see if duplication can be of assistance. In *diagram 152* White throws 4:2. His opponent must use any 1 or 4 for re-entry, therefore the safest places to leave blots will be 1 and/or 4 points away from the black men. White therefore moves B5–B11 with one man as in

DIAGRAM 146

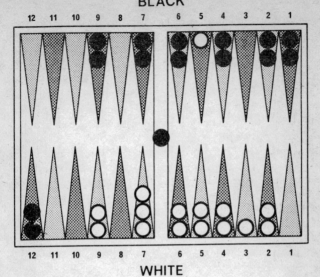

DIAGRAM 147

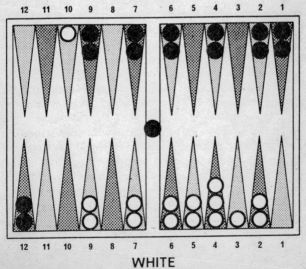

DIAGRAM 148

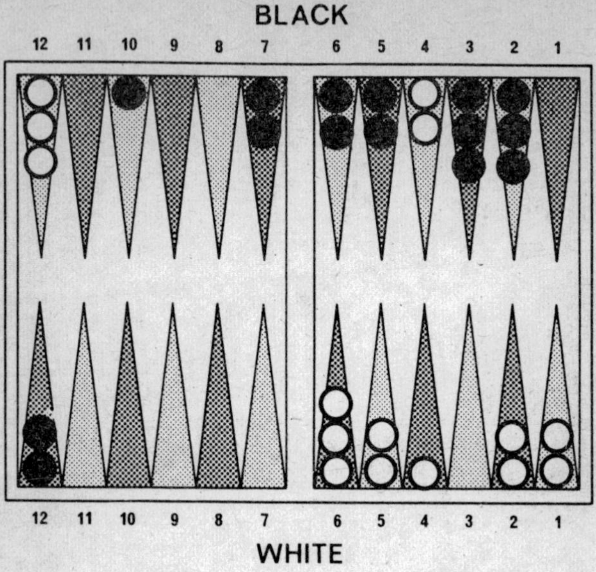

BLACK

| 12 | 11 | 10 | 9 | 8 | 7 | 6 | 5 | 4 | 3 | 2 | 1 |

WHITE

DIAGRAM 149

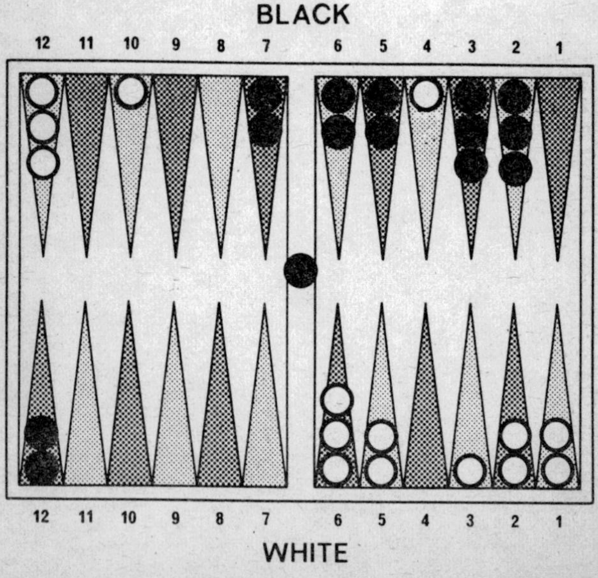

BLACK

| 12 | 11 | 10 | 9 | 8 | 7 | 6 | 5 | 4 | 3 | 2 | 1 |

WHITE

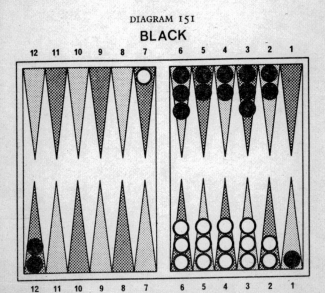

DIAGRAM 152

BLACK

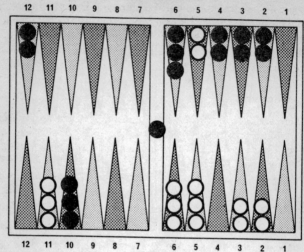

WHITE

DIAGRAM 153

BLACK

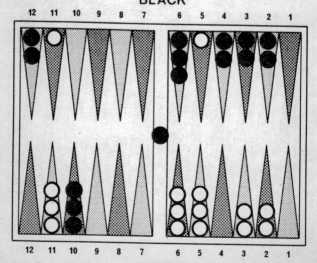

WHITE

diagram 153 where it can only be hit by a 1 or 4. The other blot, on B5, can also only be hit by a 1. Note how White did not move both men to B7 and B9 where they could be hit by a 6, 5 or 3; none of these numbers is required for re-entry and they are therefore available to hit blots.

Non-duplication

There are occasions when non-duplication is just as important as duplication. In *diagram 154* White must at all costs stop Black escaping. If he escapes he will run for home and be in a winning position. White has just thrown 5:1. He hits with the 5, moving W7–W2, but how does he play the 1? White must work on the assumption that Black will re-enter and hit the blot. If this happens then White will be forced to use any 5 for re-entry,

DIAGRAM 154

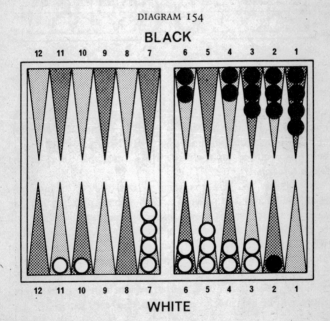

DIAGRAM 155
BLACK

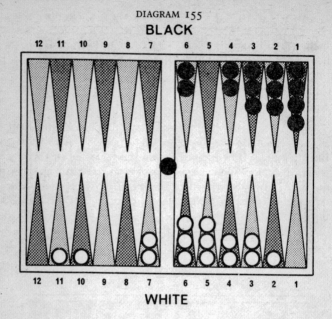

WHITE

so that the spare man on W7 will not be available to re-hit the black blot. So he now selects his move for the 1 on the principle of non-duplication and moves W7–W6. Now 3 or 4, neither of which is required for re-entry, will be available for re-hitting Black (*diagram 155*).

In *diagram 156* White is going all out to close up his home board and has just thrown 6:4. He cannot cover his blot, so again he must plan his moves on the assumption that Black will re-enter and hit the blot on his next turn. Should this happen White will need any 5, 3 or 2 for re-entry. Therefore he must place his men in positions where they can re-hit the black blot with 6, 4 or 1. White plays W8–W2 with the 6, and W9–W5 with the 5. Now any 1 or 4, neither of which are required for re-entry, will be available to hit on W1 (*diagram 157*).

DIAGRAM 156

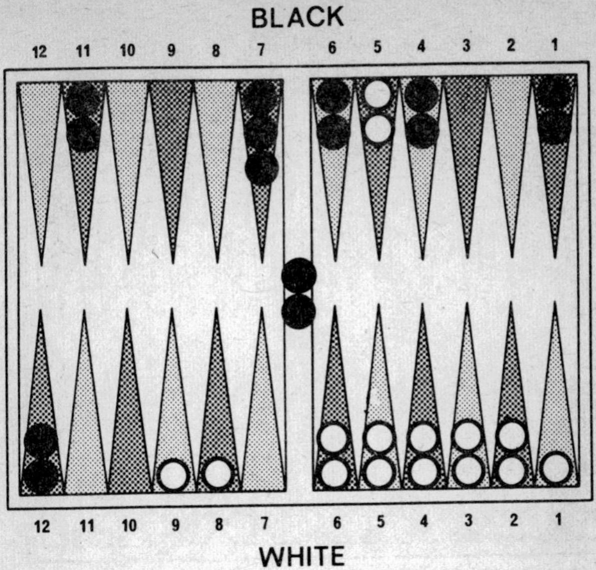

BLACK

WHITE

DIAGRAM 157

BLACK

WHITE

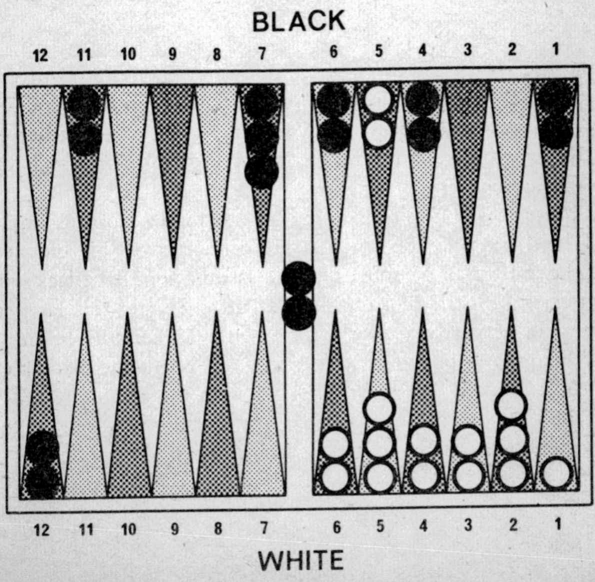

DIAGRAM 158

BLACK

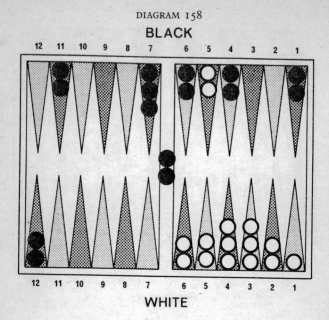

WHITE

In contrast look now at the same move played incorrectly, as in *diagram 158*. Here White has played W9–W3, W8–W4. In this position he could only re-hit on W1 with a 2 or 3, both of which are numbers that may be needed for re-entry and may not therefore be available for hitting the blot.

The uninitiated backgammon player will not notice the difference in these two moves. At first sight they both look as though they give two builders with which to re-hit the blot, and when the second move fails to hit, the innocent player may well blame his bad luck rather than his lack of skill!

In chess it is necessary to think many moves ahead. In contrast, because backgammon is based on the unexpected dice, many players think that there is no need to think of the next throw of the dice; but as seen in this last example, it is necessary

DIAGRAM 159

BLACK

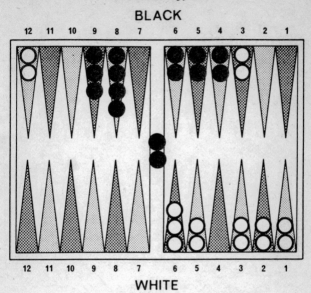

WHITE

to think ahead by two turns, one for your opponent and one for you.

Diagram 159 is another example of non-duplication. White has just thrown 3:2. How should he play it? White has two considerations:

1 To bring up his builders to enhance his chances of hitting any Black blot that manages to re-enter on W4.
2 He must escape with his last two men from the black home board.

If White moves one man B12–W8 with his 3:2 he will only be able to hit on W4 with a 4. This he cannot allow to happen, since every 4 that he gets will be needed to remove his men from the black home board. He must move his men so that a hit is

DIAGRAM 160

BLACK

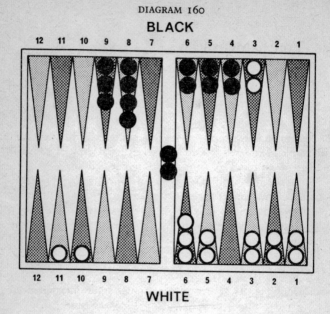

WHITE

possible with a number other than a 4. The correct move is
B12–W10, B12–W11, as in *diagram 160*. Now all 4s can be used
to extricate his men, and any 6 will hit on W4. He will not have
reduced his chances of escape and hitting by blocking himself
with duplication of a vital move.

Duplication and non-duplication moves are a great aid in
increasing the chances of a subsequent throw being to your
advantage. They help to put the law of probability on your
side—not on your opponent's side.

contest, not money, alters your attitude and style of play. There may be prize money for the winners, but each match you play is played to win the match, not to take money off your opponent. Therefore there is no material difference between winning 11–0 and 11–10. No money changes hands, so there is no need to take risks to win by a large margin.

Use of the doubling cube in a tournament

In a 9-point match with the score 8–7 in your favour you would not double your opponent. Whether you win 9–7 or 10–7 makes not the slightest difference to the result. Your double simply adds to the risk, for should your opponent win his score will jump to 9 making him the winner of the match.

Conversely, if you are in the losing position with the score 7–8, you must double at the first opportunity, right at the beginning of the game. If you lose this game you are out of the contest, so double your opponent at the start and then if you win you win the match. This starting double puts pressure on your opponent and increases the chances of his making an error.

If the score was 7–5 in favour of your opponent in a 9-point match, and he doubled you, and assuming that you considered it correct to accept the double, then on your next turn you would re-double him to 4. Again you have nothing to lose. If you do not win you have lost the match, so force him into either conceding the game and giving you 2 points, or to play for 4 points so that if you win you win the match. A re-double of this nature is very disconcerting for your opponent.

Because of this situation where the losing player can, by wild use of the doubling cube, sometimes snatch victory from a superior player (perhaps by use of a double combined with a lucky backgammon), the Crawford rule came into existence and is now frequently used in tournaments. This rule states that when one player is one point away from victory the doubling cube cannot be used for that one game. After that game the cube may again be used as before.

This gives the player who has come close to victory a safe

game in which his opponent cannot snatch victory with a wild double.

In an elimination match you treat the doubling cube with great care, and before you use it weigh up the consequences of an instant re-double. If you are leading in the match, be very cautious and double as little as possible. If you are losing the match use it freely. The winner has to play with the greater caution and must quite frequently refuse your double to give you a point, rather than risk a 2 point loss. Hesitate to double the winner when he needs only 2 points to win as a lost game in this situation costs you the match.

If you are up against a less skilled player refuse doubles that are based on lucky situations. For example, in a running game in which the two sides have no contact (*i.e.* the men have disengaged), where the fickle dice will decide the issue, you would refuse the double. If you had been playing for money the probabilities might well make acceptance of the double the right thing to do, but in this situation you do not cast away 2 vital points on the luck of the dice. You should prefer to accept doubles where superior skill can help you.

In end game play never accept doubles if your chances are much below 50%. When playing for money you accept these doubles, not because you expect to win, but because by accepting you actually lose less money than by resigning. In a knockout tournament the law of large numbers does not apply. You can only lose once, so refuse doubles where probability is not on your side.

Tournament gammons and backgammons

A win by a backgammon is partly due to luck rather than to skill. For this reason backgammons are not very often allowed in tournaments. To a lesser extent the same can be said about gammons. This has given rise to the Jacoby rule that states that no gammon can be claimed unless a double has first been offered and accepted during the game. In other words a player must have had the opportunity of resigning by refusing the double, and only if he does not resign may the gammon count. This rule forces players to be even more cautious with the doubling cube as the loss of a doubled gammon is a painful experience.

The rules governing gammons and backgammons clearly have a major effect on the way you play. If none are allowed, or if the Jacoby rule applies you can risk playing a back game, or waiting in your opponent's home board for a shot at him. If he doubles you, resignation and the loss of 1 point is not too costly, but as long as he does not double you, you can remain waiting for the lucky shot that might save you. If, however, gammons and backgammons do apply, or if there is no Jacoby rule, never risk a situation where you will be gammoned or backgammoned. In an elimination match you cannot afford to lose 2 or 3 points in one game. You never play a back game, preferring instead to run and lose one point.

Three final tips

1 **Scoring:** When playing in a tournament make sure that at the end of each game you and your opponent agree on the score and that you both record the result. Many disputes arise if one or other of the players has been careless in recording the result.

2 **Watching:** If you win your round, do not wait about to be called for the next round. Go to the results board and find out who you will be playing next. If they are still playing go and watch them at play, you may gain clues that will enable you to win.

3 **Spectators:** If a spectator is annoying you, or is in some way making helpful noises to attract your opponent's attention to incorrect play, do not hesitate to ask that he be removed. Most tournaments have rules that make it proper for a judge to remove spectators who cause annoyance. It is far better to have him removed, rather than allowing him to rattle you with his intrusions, whatever form they may take.

10   Chouette

Backgammon for 3 to 6 players.

Chouette is a social form of backgammon whereby a family, or a group of people, can all partake in the game despite the fact there is only one backgammon board available.

This chapter describes the basic version of chouette and does not go into the more complicated arrangements and deals that can take place when the game is played by experienced and hardened gamblers.

To start a game of Chouette all players roll one die each. The person getting the highest number goes into 'the box'. The remainder of the players form a team to play against the box, so that the result of the initial dice casting is as follows:

> The highest die   —Wins the box
> The 2nd highest die—Becomes Captain of the team
> The 3rd highest die —Becomes No. 1 Adviser
> The 4th highest die —Becomes No. 2 Adviser
> The 5th highest die —Becomes No. 3 Adviser
> The 6th highest die —Becomes No. 4 Adviser

If any two or more players throw the same number, they each re-throw their dice until an order of precedence is established as above.

Everyone in the team is playing against the lone man in the box. The game proceeds in exactly the same way as any normal game of backgammon. The player in the box throws his dice and plays his moves. The Captain of the team throws his dice and plays the moves for the team.

The Captain of the team has the right to decide on a definite move and to impose his decision on his team, if necessary. The rest of the team have the right to give advice and make suggestions to the Captain. The Captain does not have to take their advice, but will certainly listen to it when any difficult decisions are involved. To save wasting time he rarely consults his team on straightforward moves and situations.

If the man in the box wins the game he remains in the box for the next game. The team having lost, now demote their Captain, who goes to the bottom of the team to become No. 4 Adviser. All the other Advisers move up one place, and the former No. 1 Adviser now becomes the new Captain.

If the man in the box wins again, exactly the same process takes place, the disgraced Captain is demoted to the lowest Adviser, and everyone moves up one place to again take on the box under a new Captain.

If the box loses, the Captain of the winning team now takes over the box, and becomes the lone player taking on everyone else. The team all move up one place, the No. 1 Adviser becoming the new Captain, and the defeated man from the box now joins the team as the lowest Adviser.

In this way everyone in the group partakes in the game of Chouette and the team always have a new Captain for each game.

Scoring in Chouette

Each member of the team scores in exactly the same way as in normal backgammon. If an undoubled game is won each member of the team records $+1$ against his name. If a doubled game is won each member of the team records $+2$ against his name, *etc.*

The difference comes with the man in the box. If he loses the game he records -1 for each member of the team. In this case where the team consists of 5 people, he records -5 or, if the game was doubled, -10.

Equally if the box wins, each member of the team records -1, and the man in the box wins 1 point from each player to become $+5$ or $+10$, as the case may be.

Recording the score

The score in Chouette can quickly degenerate into complete chaos unless it is carefully recorded at the end of each game. Normally one record sheet is kept and will look like this, but with each player's name at the top.

		A	B	C	D	E	F
Game 1	Box (A) beats team under Capt. B. Capt. B demoted	+5	−1	−1	−1	−1	−1
Game 2	Box (A) beats team under Capt. C, doubled. Capt. C demoted	+10	−2	−2	−2	−2	−2
		—	—	—	—	—	—
		+15	−3	−3	−3	−3	−3
Game 3	Box (A) loses doubled and gammoned to team under Capt. D. D now takes over box	−20	+4	+4	+4	+4	+4
		—	—	—	—	—	—
		−5	+1	+1	+1	+1	+1
Game 4	Box (D) wins doubled against team under Capt. E. Capt. E demoted	−2	−2	−2	+10	−2	−2
		—	—	—	—	—	—
	Final score:	−7	−1	−1	+11	−1	−1

Note that after the results of each game have been recorded the total of the plus points always equals the total of the minus points. This must be checked after each game to make sure that no errors have crept into the record.

When the game of Chouette comes to an end each player who has lost money pays up his losses, and the winners collect their winnings.

Doubles in Chouette

Doubles in Chouette are exactly the same as in backgammon. On being doubled the man in the box, or the team, have the right to accept or refuse. The complication arises when the team disagree, some being for accepting, some for refusing. Those members of the team who do not want to accept can refuse the double, record against their names the appropriate minus, and against the name of the man in the box the appropriate plus.

The game now proceeds with the remaining members of the team who accepted playing against the box. The members of the team who refused the double may not now give any advice until a new game starts.

If the Captain accepted the double, he continues as Captain. If, however, he was amongst those refusing the double, the job of Captain falls on the next-highest-ranking player who accepted. Should the team win, the man who was Captain at the time of the win moves into the box. The ex-Captain, who made the error of not accepting the double, goes down to the bottom of the team, and the defeated man from the box joins the team below him.

The other players, whether they accepted the double or not, resume their same places in the team for the next game.

If the members of the team who accepted the double lose, no one loses his position in the team. The game proceeds as normal; the original Captain, not the temporary Captain who accepted the double, moves to the bottom of the team.

The man in the box

In Chouette, everyone who has any gambling instincts always wants to be in the box, where, if you win, you collect money from five different people—or in other words your wins are multiplied five times compared to playing a game against a single opponent for the same stake. BUT, when you lose you also lose five times as much!

Therefore it is in the interests of the team to double, very freely. It does not cost each individual member very much when they lose, but by comparison, when the box loses it costs a fortune. By doubling the box freely the team hope that the fear of a big loss will make the man in the box resign early to keep his losses as low as possible, and therefore add to the profit for the members of the team.

When you are in the box, be very sure before you offer a double. If the team see any hope they will come straight back with a re-double, and though you cannot afford the loss, they, with five of them to share it, can.

As long as you are in the box be very slow to double, and if you have possession of the cube, keep it that way until you have a near watertight position.

Lastly, if, while you are in the box, you have been fortunate and skillful enough to make some big wins, do not hesitate to resign when you are offered a double in a weak position. Why take a risky double and risk your wins? Get out while the going is good, take your wins with you when you rejoin the team, not losses. The bigger your wins the more cautious you must become to protect them.

A word of warning

Before you join a game of Chouette, get the question of automatic doubles in all its forms clearly settled. If you get in the box in a game with unlimited automatic doubles, beavers, and other methods of rotating the cube upwards, one loss can cost you a fortune. Always get the automatic double situation quite clear before you join the game.

So long as you are not out of your depth financially, playing Chouette with players better than yourself is one of the best ways of learning more about backgammon. If you do not want to risk being in the box (with the accompanying dangers of high losses) you have the right to pass it onto the next man in the team, whilst you move down to the bottom of the team.

11 Tables of Opening Moves and Responses

The following tables are not intended to list the best opening moves, and the best responses to each opening move; instead a choice of moves is given to encourage beginners to experiment with running moves, blocking moves, *etc.* and to find out for themselves the best style of play to defeat different opponents.

In each group of opening moves one move has a star (★) against it. This star indicates that the responses to this move are listed in the table of responses that follow.

In this first table of opening moves, all moves are quoted for White.

TABLE OF OPENING MOVES FOR WHITE

Dice Combinations	No. of Men Moved	From	To
6–5 ★	1	B1	B12 ★
6–4 (A) ★	1	B1	B11 ★
or (B)	1 ⎱	B1	B7
	1 ⎰	B12	W9
or (C)	1 ⎱	B12	W7
	1 ⎰	B12	W9
6–3 (A)	1	B1	B10
or (B)	1 ⎱	B12	W7
	1 ⎰	B12	W10
or (C) ★	1 ⎱	B1	B7 ★
	1 ⎰	B12	W10

Dice Combinations	No. of Men Moved	From	To
6–2 (A)★	I	B12	W5★
or (B)	I ⎱ I ⎰	B1 B12	B7 W11
or (C)	I ⎱ I ⎰	B12 B12	W11 W7
6–1 ★	I ⎱ I ⎰	B12 W8	W7★ W7
5–4 (A)	I ⎱ I ⎰	B12 B12	W8 W9
or (B)★	I ⎱ I ⎰	B12 B1	W8★ B5
or (C)	I	B1	B10
5–3 (A)★	I ⎱ I ⎰	B12 B12	W8★ W10
or (B)	I	B12	W5
or (C)	I	B1	B9
5–2 ★	I ⎱ I ⎰	B12 B12	W8★ W11
5–1 (A)	I ⎱ I ⎰	B12 W6	W8 W5
or (B)★	I ⎱ I ⎰	B1 B12	B2★ W8
4–3 (A)★	I ⎱ I ⎰	B12 B12	W9★ W10
or (B)	I ⎱ I ⎰	B1 B12	B5 W10
4–2 ★	I ⎱ I ⎰	W8 W6	W4★ W4

Dice Combinations	No. of Men Moved	From	To
4–1 (A)	1 ⎫ 1 ⎭	W6 B12	W5 W9
or (B)★	1 ⎫ 1 ⎭	B1 B12	B2 ★ W9
3–2 ★	1 ⎫ 1 ⎭	B12 B12	W11 W10
3–1 ★	1 ⎫ 1 ⎭	W8 W6	W5 W5
2–1 (A)★	1 ⎫ 1 ⎭	W6 B12	W5 ★ W11
or (B)	1 ⎫ 1 ⎭	B1 B12	B2 W11

Tables of responses to the opening move

It is virtually impossible to list all possible responses to all the different opening moves. This table gives one possible response for each dice combination for the opening moves marked with a star (★).

Beginners should at first use the opening move with a star, and select the response from the tables below. Once familiar with these moves they should experiment with different opening moves and devise their own response.

Readers will observe that the responses quoted vary. This is done deliberately, so that the beginners realise that the same dice combination often has more than one good movement.

In the table of responses below, the opening move is for Black and the responses are for White.

Opening move 6:5   Move 1 man W1–W12

Response   For all dice combinations play your response as though you were the opener.

Opening move 6:4   Move 1 man W1–W11

Response (for White)

6:6	2 men B12–W7	2 men B1–B7
6:5	1 man B1–B12	
6:4	1 man B1–B7	1 man B12–W9
6:3	1 man B1–B7	1 man B12–W10
6:2	1 man B1–B7	1 man B12–W11 (*hit blot*)
6:1	1 man B12–W7	1 man W8–W7
5:5	2 men B12–W3	
5:4	1 man B12–W8	1 man B1–B5
5:3	1 man B12–W8	1 man B12–W10
5:2	1 man B12–W8	1 man B12–W11 (*hit blot*)
5:1	1 man B12–W8	1 man B1–B2
4:4	2 men B12–W5	
4:3	1 man B12–W10	1 man B1–B5
4:2	1 man W8–W4	1 man W6–W4
4:1	1 man B12–W9	1 man W6–W5
3:3	2 men B12–W10	2 men W8–W5
3:2	1 man B12–W10	1 man B12–W11 (*hit blot*)
3:1	1 man W8–W5	1 man W6–W5
2:2	2 men W6–W4	2 men B12–W11 (*hit blot*)
2:1	1 man B1–B2	1 man B12–W11 (*hit blot*)
1:1	2 men W8–W7	2 men W6–W5

Opening move 6:3   Move 1 man W1–W7, 1 man W12–B10

Response

6:6	2 men B1–B7	2 men B12–W7 (*hit blot*)
6:5	1 man B12–W8	1 man B12–W7 (*hit blot*)
6:4	1 man B12–W9	1 man B12–W7 (*hit blot*)
6:3	1 man B1–B10 (*hit blot*)	
6:2	1 man B12–W11	1 man B12–W7 (*hit blot*)
6:1	1 man B12–W7	1 man W8–W7 (*hit blot*)
5:5	2 men B12–W3	
5:4	1 man B1–B10 (*hit blot*)	
5:3	1 man W8–W3	1 man W6–W3

5:2	1 man B12–W8	1 man B1–B3
5:1	1 man B12–W8	1 man W8–W7 (*hit blot*)
4:4	2 men B12–W5	
4:3	1 man W8–W1 (*hit blot*)	
4:2	1 man W8–W4	1 man W6–W4
4:1	1 man B1–B5	1 man W8–W7 (*hit blot*)
3:3	2 men W8–W5	1 man B12–W7 (*hit blot*)
3:2	1 man W6–W1 (*hit blot*)	
3:1	1 man W8–W5	1 man W6–W5
2:2	2 men B12–W11	2 men W6–W4
2:1	1 man B12–W11	1 man W8–W7 (*hit blot*)
1:1	2 men W6–W5	2 men W8–W7 (*hit blot*)

Opening move 6:2   Move 1 man W12–B5

Response

6:6	2 men B1–B7	2 men B12–W7
6:5	1 man B1–B12	
6:4	1 man B1–B11 (*hit blot*)	
6:3	1 man B1–B7	1 man B12–W10
6:2	1 man B12–W5	
6:1	1 man B12–W7	1 man W8–W7
5:5	2 men B12–W3	
5:4	1 man B12–W8	1 man B1–B5 (*hit blot*)
5:3	1 man B12–W8	1 man B12–W10
5:2	1 man B12–W8	1 man B12–W11
5:1	1 man B12–W8	1 man B1–B2
4:4	2 men B12–W9	2 men B1–B5 (*hit blot*)
4:3	1 man B12–W10	1 man B1–B5 (*hit blot*)
4:2	1 man W8–W4	1 man W6–W4
4:1	1 man B1–B2	1 man B1–B5 (*hit blot*)
3:3	2 men W8–W5	2 men W6–W3
3:2	1 man B12–W10	1 man B12–W11
3:1	1 man W8–W5	1 man W6–W5
2:2	2 men W6–W4	1 man B1–B5 (*hit blot*)
2:1	1 man B1–B2	1 man B12–W11
1:1	2 men W8–W7	2 men W6–W5

Opening move 6:1   Move 1 man W12–B7, and 1 man B8–B7

Response

6:6	2 men B12–W7	2 men W8–W2
6:5	1 man B12–W7	1 man B12–W8
6:4	1 man B1–B11	
6:3	1 man B1–B10	
6:2	1 man B1–B9	
6:1	1 man B12–W7	1 man W8–W7
5:5	2 men B12–W3	
5:4	1 man B1–B5	1 man B12–W8
5:3	1 man B12–W8	1 man B12–W10
5:2	1 man B12–W8	1 man B12–W11
5:1	1 man B12–W8	1 man W6–W5
4:4	2 men B1–B5	2 men B12–W9
4:3	1 man B1–B5	1 man B12–W10
4:2	1 man W8–W4	1 man W6–W4
4:1	1 man B1–B5	1 man B1–B2
3:3	2 men W8–W5	2 men B1–B4
3:2	1 man B12–W11	1 man B12–W10
3:1	1 man W8–W5	1 man W6–W5
2:2	2 men B1–B3	2 men W6–W4
2:1	1 man B12–W11	1 man W6–W5
1:1	2 men W8–W7	2 men W6–W5

Opening move 5:4   Move 1 man W12–B8 and 1 man W1–W5

Response

6:6	2 men B1–B7	2 men B12–W7
6:5	1 man B1–B12	
6:4	1 man B1–B7	1 man B1–B5
6:3	1 man B1–B10	
6:2	1 man B1–B9	
6:1	1 man B12–W7	1 man W8–W7
5:5	2 men B12–W3	
5:4	1 man B12–W8	1 man B1–B5

5:3	1 man B1–B9	
5:2	1 man B12–W8	1 man B1–B3
5:1	1 man B12–W8	1 man B1–B2
4:4	2 men B12–W5 (*hit blot*)	
4:3	1 man B1–B5	1 man B1–B4
4:2	1 man W8–W4	1 man W6–W4
4:1	1 man B1–B2	1 man B1–B5
3:3	2 men W6–W3	2 men W8–W5 (*hit blot*)
3:2	1 man Б1–B3	1 man B1–B4
3:1	1 man W8–W5	1 man W6–W5 (*hit blot*)
2:2	2 men B12–W11	2 men W6–W4
2:1	1 man B1–B2	1 man B1–B3
1:1	2 men W8–W7	2 men W6–W5 (*hit blot*)

Opening move 5:3   Move 1 man W12–B8, and 1 man W12–B10

Response

6:6	2 men B1–B7	2 men B12–W7
6:5	1 man B1–B12	
6:4	1 man B1–B11	
6:3	1 man B1–B10 (*hit blot*)	
6:2	1 man B12–W5	
6:1	1 man B12–W7	1 man W8–W7
5:5	2 men B12–W3	
5:4	1 man B1–B10 (*hit blot*)	
5:3	1 man B12–W8	1 man B12–W10
5:2	1 man B12–W8	1 man B12–W11
5:1	1 man B12–W8	1 man B1–B2
4:4	2 men B12–W5	
4:3	1 man B12–W9	1 man B12–W10
4:2	1 man W8–W4	1 man W6–W4
4:1	1 man B12–W9	1 man B1–B2
3:3	2 men W8–W5	2 men W6–W3
3:2	1 man B12–W10	1 man B12–W11
3:1	1 man W8–W5	1 man W6–W5

2:2	2 men W6–W4	2 men B12–W11
2:1	1 man B12–W11	1 man W6–W5
1:1	2 men W8–W7	2 men W6–W5

Opening move 5:2   Move 1 man W12–B8, and 1 man W12–B11

Response

6:6	2 men B1–B7	2 men B12–W7
6:5	1 man B1–B12	
6:4	1 man B1–B11 (*hit blot*)	
6:3	1 man B1–B10	
6:2	1 man B12–W5	
6:1	1 man B12–W7	1 man W8–W7
5:5	2 men B12–W3	
5:4	1 man B12–W8	1 man B12–W9
5:3	1 man B12–W8	1 man B12–W10
5:2	1 man B12–W8	1 man B12–W11
5:1	1 man B12–W8	1 man B1–B2
4:4	2 men B12–W5	
4:3	1 man B1–B4	1 man B12–W9
4:2	1 man W8–W4	1 man W6–W4
4:1	1 man B12–W9	1 man B1–B2
3:3	2 men W8–W5	2 men W6–W3
3:2	1 man W8–W5	1 man B12–W11
3:1	1 man W8–W5	1 man W6–W5
2:2	2 men W6–W4	2 men B12–W11
2:1	1 man B12–W11	1 man B1–B2
1:1	2 men W8–W7	2 men W6–W5

Opening move 5:1   Move 1 man W1–W2 and 1 man W12–B8

Response For all dice combinations play your response as though you were the opener, but avoid leaving blots on W5–W7.

Opening move 4:3   Move 1 man W12–B9, and 1 man W12–B10

Response

6:6	2 men B1–B7	2 men B12–W7
6:5	1 man B1–B12	
6:4	1 man B1–B11	
6:3	1 man B1–B10 (*hit blot*)	
6:2	1 man B1–B9 (*hit blot*)	
6:1	1 man B12–W7	1 man W8–W7
5:5	2 men B12–W3	
5:4	1 man B1–B10 (*hit blot*)	
5:3	1 man B1–B9 (*hit blot*)	
5:2	1 man B12–W8	1 man B12–W11
5:1	1 man B12–W8	1 man B1–B2
4:4	2 men W8–W4	1 man B1–B9 (*hit blot*)
4:3	1 man B12–W10	1 man B12–W9
4:2	1 man W8–W4	1 man W6–W4
4:1	1 man B12–W9	1 man B1–B2
3:3	2 men W8–W5	2 men B1–B4
3:2	1 man B12–W10	1 man B12–W11
3:1	1 man W8–W5	1 man W6–W5
2:2	2 men W6–W4	2 men B1–B3
2:1	1 man B12–W11	1 man B1–B2
1:1	2 men W8–W7	2 men W6–W5

Opening move 4:2   Move 1 man B8–B4 and 1 man B6–B4

Response

6:6	2 men B1–B7	2 men B12–W7
6:5	1 man B1–B12	
6:4	1 man B1–B11	
6:3	1 man B1–B10	
6:2	1 man B1–B9	
6:1	1 man B12–W7	1 man W8–W7
5:5	2 men B12–W3	
5:4	1 man B1–B5	1 man B12–W8

5:3	1 man B12–W8	1 man B12–W10
5:2	1 man B12–W8	1 man B12–W11
5:1	1 man B12–W8	1 man W6–W5
4:4	2 men B1–B5	2 men B12–W9
4:3	1 man B1–B5	1 man B12–W10
4:2	1 man W8–W4	1 man W6–W4
4:1	1 man B12–W9	1 man W6–W5
3:3	2 men W8–W5	2 men B12–W10
3:2	1 man B12–W10	1 man B12–W11
3:1	1 man W8–W5	1 man W6–W5
2:2	2 men B1–B5	
2:1	1 man B12–W11	1 man W6–W5
1:1	2 men W8–W7	2 men W6–W5

Opening move 4:1   Move 1 man W12–B9, and 1 man W1–W2

Response

6:6	2 men B1–B7	2 men B12–W7
6:5	1 man B1–B12	
6:4	1 man B1–B11	
6:3	1 man B1–B10	
6:2	1 man B1–B9 (*hit blot*)	
6:1	1 man B12–W7	1 man W8–W7
5:5	2 men B12–W3	
5:4	1 man B12–W8	1 man B12–W9
5:3	1 man B1–B9 (*hit blot*)	
5:2	1 man B12–W8	1 man B12–W11
5:1	1 man B12–W8	1 man B1–B2
4:4	2 men B12–W9	1 man B1–B9 (*hit blot*)
4:3	1 man B1–B5	1 man B12–W10
4:2	1 man W8–W4	1 man W6–W4
4:1	1 man W6–W1 (*hit 2 blots*)	
3:3	2 men B12–W10	2 men W8–W5
3:2	1 man B1–B4	1 man B12–W11
3:1	1 man W8–W5	1 man W6–W5

2:2	2 men B12–W11	2 men W6–W4
2:1	1 man B1–B2	1 man B12–W11
1:1	2 men W8–W7	2 men W6–W5

Opening move 3:2   Move 1 man W12–B11, and 1 man W12–B10

Response

6:6	2 men B1–B7	2 men B12–W7
6:5	1 man B1–B12	
6:4	1 man B1–B11 (*hit blot*)	
6:3	1 man B1–B10 (*hit blot*)	
6:2	1 man B12–W5	
6:1	1 man B12–W7	1 man W8–W7
5:5	2 men B12–W3	
5:4	1 man B1–W10 (*hit blot*)	
5:3	1 man B12–W8	1 man B12–W10
5:2	1 man B12–W8	1 man B12–W11
5:1	1 man B12–W8	1 man B1–B2
4:4	2 men B12–W9	2 men B1–B5
4:3	1 man B12–W9	1 man B12–W10
4:2	1 man W8–W4	1 man W6–W4
4:1	1 man B12–W9	1 man B1–B2
3:3	2 men W8–W5	2 men B1–B4
3:2	1 man B12–W10	1 man B12–W11
3:1	1 man W8–W5	1 man W6–W5
2:2	2 men B12–W11	2 men B1–B3
2:1	1 man B12–W11	1 man W6–W5
1:1	2 men W8–W7	2 men W6–W5

Opening move 3:1   Move 1 man B8–B5 and 1 man B6–B5

Response

6:6	2 men B1–B7	2 men B12–W7
6:5	1 man B1–B12	
6:4	1 man B1–B11	
6:3	1 man B1–B10	

6:2	1 man B12–W5	
6:1	1 man B12–W7	1 man W8–W7
5:5	2 men B12–W3	
5:4	1 man B12–W8	1 man B12–W9
5:3	1 man B12–W8	1 man B12–W10
5:2	1 man B12–W8	1 man B12–W11
5:1	1 man B12–W8	1 man W6–W5
4:4	2 men B12–W5	
4:3	1 man B12–W9	1 man B12–W10
4:2	1 man W8–W4	1 man W6–W4
4:1	1 man B12–W9	1 man W6–W5
3:3	2 men W8–W5	2 men B1–B4
3:2	1 man B12–W10	1 man B12–W11
3:1	1 man W8–W5	1 man W6–W5
2:2	2 men B1–B3	2 men W6–W4
2:1	1 man B12–W11	1 man W6–W5
1:1	2 men W8–W7	2 men W6–W5

Opening move 2:1   Move 1 man W12–B11 and 1 man B6–B5

Response

6:6	2 men B1–B7	2 men B12–W7
6:5	1 man B1–B12	
6:4	1 man B1–B11 (*hit 2 blots*)	
6:3	1 man B1–B10	
6:2	1 man B12–W5	
6:1	1 man B12–W7	1 man W8–W7
5:5	2 men B12–W3	
5:4	1 man B12–W8	1 man B1–B5 (*hit blot*)
5:3	1 man B12–W8	1 man B12–W10
5:2	1 man B12–W8	1 man B12–W11
5:1	1 man B12–W8	1 man B1–B2
4:4	2 men B12–W9	2 men B1–B5 (*hit blot*)
4:3	1 man B12–W10	1 man B1–B5 (*hit blot*)
4:2	1 man B12–W11	1 man B1–B5 (*hit blot*)

4:1	1 man B1–B2	1 man B1–B5 (*hit blot*)
3:3	2 men W8–W5	2 men B1–B4
3:2	1 man B12–W10	1 man B12–W11
3:1	1 man W8–W5	1 man W6–W5
2:2	2 men W6–W4	1 man B1–B5 (*hit blot*)
2:1	1 man B12–W11	1 man B1–B2
1:1	2 men W8–W7	2 men W6–W5

Introducing the World's Most Respected View on Games

Quite simply *Games & Puzzles* is unique. There is no other publication quite like it anywhere in the world.

Started four years ago by a small team of games experts, games inventors and journalists who were games devotees, *Games & Puzzles* has since grown substantially to become recognised throughout the world as the leading authority on games, games inventions and games playing.

The magazine is witty, entertaining and most of all objective and highly informed. So if you're interested in playing, inventing or even making games, it's the one publication in the world you really can't afford to miss.

Special Introductory Offer

For new subscribers we offer a 3-months' trial period so you can vouch for yourself that our magazine is really all we claim. If, during your initial 3-month period, you wish to cancel your subscription, we will immediately refund you your money in full. Please write enclosing your subscription (cheque/money order/postal order) to:

> Circulation Manager,
> *Games & Puzzles*,
> 11 Tottenham Court Road,
> London W1A 4XF

Subscription rates:

	One Year	Three Years
United Kingdom	£4.80	£14.40
USA/Canada	$12.00	$36.00
Other Countries	£5.40	£16.20